D0800360

Maximize Your Social Security

Philip Wilson

CLTC, CEA, CSSCS, CCPS

Copyright © 2019 Philip Wilson

ALL RIGHTS RESERVED. This book contains material protected under International and Federal Copyright Laws and Treaties. Any unauthorized reprint or use of this material is prohibited. No part of this book may be reproduced or transmitted in any form or by any means, electronic or mechanical, including photocopying, recording, or by any information storage and retrieval system, without express written permission from the author/publisher.

ISBN:
Paperback: 978-1-64184-106-1
Ebook: 978-1-64184-107-8

Required Disclosure:

Philip is the founder of Wilson Financial Group which is a fee-only Alabama Registered Investment Advisor. For residents of other states in which registration is not held, proper registrations must be obtained by Philip Wilson before proceeding further, and any requests for information or service may be delayed. No part of this communication should be construed as an offer to sell any security or provide investment advice or recommendation. Check the background of this investment professional on FINRA's BrokerCheck.

Dedicated to Rhonda, Matthew and Caroline,
my reasons for getting out of bed every day.

TABLE OF CONTENTS

CHAPTER 1

Lifetime Income

The Social Security decision can be described in several different ways. One way is by calling it the most important financial decision you will make in your lifetime. Specifically, I am referring to the decision of when and how you file for Social Security benefits as being the most important financial decision you will make in your lifetime. Most people would think filing for Social Security is important but not necessarily *the* most important financial decision in your lifetime. So, let me explain.

Retirement planning has always been a daunting task. Preparing for slowing down requires a good amount of planning and resources. For this generation, however, there are some unique challenges. This generation of retirees will be the first in history to spend more time in retirement than they do working.

Other factors such as rising health care costs, the rising cost of nursing homes and home health care, and the elimination of employer-provided pensions, challenge the retiree as never before.

A further complication is low interest rates that come with "safe" returns, thus requiring more principal to provide the necessary income for retirement. Retires are at more risk than ever of outliving their assets and possibly becoming dependent upon others or the government to take care of them. We will all be frail at some point in our lives. Will we have the resources to take care of us?

The most crucial element to successful retirement planning today is lifetime income. Lifetime income is a source of income that lasts for your lifetime. It last as long as you last. I describe it as an infinite asset because it never runs out and always provides income. You cannot outlive it regardless of whether you live to age 75 or 175. It is crucial for a successful retirement for an obvious reason: we are living longer and will need more assets due to the number of years spent in retirement. Today's retiree, if they do not have lifetime income, may outlive their assets.

To truly appreciate the value of lifetime income, you need to convert a stream of income into the amount of principal needed to produce the income. Consider a lifetime stream of $15,000 of annual income and suppose this continues for 20 years. It would take $300,000 of principal to produce this income over that period.

Suppose the $15,000 of income was increased for inflation. This would not only double the income over the 20 years, it would also double the amount of principal necessary to produce the income over the 20 years. Inflation-adjusted income is income that increases with inflation year after year depending on the amount of inflation that year.

Social Security has always been the largest source of retirement income for most people, and now it is the only source of lifetime income for the retiree and their only source of inflation-adjusted lifetime income. This is because in recent decades, employers have shifted the retirement savings burden to employees.

Long gone are the days of working for an employer and retiring on a pension. Any income you need to retire must be saved by you. The burden for being prepared for retirement is on you, not on your employer.

Did you take advantage of your employer's 401K plan?

Do you have an IRA?

Are you behind in saving for retirement?

The great fear of anyone in retirement is running out of assets and becoming dependent upon someone else to take care of them. We need more and more assets than ever not to become dependent upon the government or someone else to take care of us when we are old. Today's retiree will spend more years in retirement than working, and this has never happened in history. Most retirees have not saved enough assets and will run out if they live a long life in retirement.

The best way to prevent running out of money is to have sources of inflation-adjusted lifetime income. This is the best protection for the retiree not to run out of assets. The Social Security filing decision is crucial because it is the largest source of retirement income for retirees. As companies phase out pensions, Social Security has now become the only source of lifetime income available to most retirees.

The true dollar value of Social Security is not appreciated by the general public. Social Security is an inflation-adjusted, guaranteed source of lifetime income. The amount of principal needed to duplicate Social Security's income makes it the largest asset for most people. The size of the asset necessary to provide inflation-adjusted, guaranteed income for life, at today's interest rates, is significant.

The challenge with Social Security benefits is that over 90% of retirees applying for benefits do not receive the maximum amount they are eligible to claim. Nine out of ten people work their entire life, pay into the system whether they want to or not, reach retirement, and do not receive the full amount of benefits available to them. So, the largest amount of retirement income and the only source of lifetime income for retirement, is not being maximized. This is why I call it the most important financial decision you will make in your lifetime. If you don't file correctly, it is like missing out on $500,000 or more in assets for retirement.

How is it possible that nine out of ten people do not receive their maximum benefit? The reason is complexity. Most people do not know the Social Security Administration has almost 3,000 filing rules and over 500 ways that you can file for benefits. Most people think there's only one decision that must be made for Social Security, namely, the age at which you should file. When you decide the age to file, it determines how much benefit you will receive. The public is just not aware of the different filing strategies that will affect the amount they receive. It is not just tied to age.

But the complexity alone is not the only reason for confusion. The rules, while challenging, are only part of the problem. The biggest reason people make this mistake is that they do not know what they don't know. Of the 90% who do not receive their maximum benefit, almost 100% of them never have a clue and never discover they left money on the table.

To make matters worse, the Social Security office does not give advice. In fact, their employees are prevented from doing so. I've had very good experiences with the Social Security office, and I think, in terms of government entities, they are one of the better ones for customer service. Most people I deal with in the offices are very passionate about what they do. They really want to help people, but they are not allowed to give advice. They are only there to answer your questions. They are not there to tell you how to file or explain the rules. They will answer your specific questions, but knowing how to file is your responsibility. They are only there to process your paperwork and determine your eligibility.

The problem is that we just don't realize their true role. Think of it this way: you don't go to the IRS for help in filing taxes, do you? If you file your taxes incorrectly, that is your fault. If you do not know the tax rules, you will pay more. Most people hire a CPA to help file. They will ask their tax advisor questions and the best way to file their return if they do not know. The CPA will bring to their attention opportunities to reduce taxes. No one would think to contact the IRS for tax help. Their job is to process your return, not to answer your tax questions or figure out the best way to reduce the taxes you owe. So why do we think the Social Security office is any different? This is where the public is making a big mistake!

Retirees do not realize there are rules, and they need to learn about filing before making the decision. They do not know where to turn for resources. They do not realize a good amount of information is necessary to make a filing decision. It is not just about deciding what age to file. The biggest mistake people make is assuming they are receiving retirement planning advice when filing for benefits from the Social Security office, or being told the best way to file for their particular situation. That is not the job of the Social Security office!

Often the retiree turns to their financial advisor or CPA for help to file and finds they do not know the rules either. It is surprising to most people their advisors do not know the Social Security rules. The financial industry goes through a lot of tests to be advisors, and we go through a lot of training and continuing education over the years. Most of this is very helpful, but very little of it has anything to do with filing for Social Security. We learn about different ways to design portfolios, different tax methods, and ways to help people save for college and set all kinds of financial goals. We learn about retirement planning. But with all the retirement planning information, very little has to do with filing for Social Security or the importance of the decision.

Most advisors never realize the importance of the Social Security decision or its value to the retiree. They don't value the benefit as they should. Their focus is on client assets, not Social Security income. I spend a lot of my time undoing recommendations other advisers provided to their clients that are just incorrect, recommendations such as filing eligibility or at what age to file. They mean well, but just do not know the rules and they have never taken the time to learn the rules.

I started my practice when I was 22. I did not know the rules for filing and did not take the time to learn them until my clients started asking me questions. Because of my age, initially most of my clients were around my age and retirement was not their focus. As they neared retirement the questions came my way. When I looked for answers, I realized there was a great deal of information needed to guide them to the right decision. It was only then that I realized my education on Social Security rules was incomplete. The certifications that exist today for Social Security planning did not exist back then. There was not really an easy way to study the 3,000 rules. Today, the available certifications in Social Security planning make the study of the rules easier. However, a lot of advisors fall into the category of the general public because these advisors do not know the complexity or importance of the decision, and never take the time to be certified. If I were to tell them it is the most important financial decision your clients will make, they would look at me like I was confused and crazy.

This book covers six major filing strategies. There are obviously many more situations involved in Social Security filing, but most of the public will fall into one or more of these six strategies. If you understand these six strategies, you'll probably not be one of the casualties, which means you should receive all the money to which you're legally entitled.

You will also notice the different strategies apply to different situations in life. Disability, widow, single, married, divorced—all require a different filing method. This is a big part of why mistakes are made, because someone files a certain way initially in retirement but needs to change because of a life event. These life events change filing strategies. Some filing strategies will apply to you while others will not, depending on your situation.

Your first and most important priority to prepare for a secure retirement is to maximize your only source of inflation-adjusted lifetime income. To do this, you need to understand the different filing strategies for Social Security. This will allow you to file correctly in order to receive all your benefits and lock in your largest source of retirement income and the only source of guaranteed, inflation-adjusted lifetime income.

Chapter 1 Summary

-   **When and how you file for Social Security benefits is the most important financial decision you will make.**

- **The most crucial element to successful retirement planning today is lifetime income.**

- **90% of retirees applying for benefits do not receive the maximum amount they are eligible to claim. Therefore, they do not lock in their largest source of retirement income and the only source of lifetime, inflation-adjusted income.**

CHAPTER 2

Waiting To File

The first and most important Social Security filing strategy to understand is the "wait to file" strategy.

This strategy asks the question: What is the optimal age to file for Social Security? Some people think you should file at age 62 because they think you might as well receive the income as early as you possibly can. The benefit is available to you at 62, why not get it? I often hear that if you file at age 62, you could invest it. Another reason is if you live a long life, you will receive it for the longest possible period. Many people claiming the benefits of filing early say they will not live a long life, often citing that their parents only lived to a certain age. Their thought process is that it will take receiving benefits to age 80 before you even breakeven, so why wait? Some argue you should file at age 62 because the Social Security Trust Fund is going to go bankrupt, so they figure they might as well get their money while they can because it's not going to be there later.

Others think you should wait to file until your normal retirement age because, if you file at age 62, the benefit is reduced by about 30%. Many people feel that it's better to have the full amount at full retirement age instead of a reduced amount at age 62. Others think the reduction is not significant and do not want to wait to file because they will have to live a long life in order for waiting to be of any benefit.

Often people think they should delay filing until age 70 because the Social Security Administration will increase your benefit from your normal retirement age by 8% per year until age 70, and that increase is very valuable to you. Other people say the increase is not that significant, it's not that beneficial to wait, and you could do a lot of other things with the income.

Popular publications have published numerous breakeven strategies based on how long you will live. These strategies suggest that if you start receiving a benefit by a certain age and continue to receive the benefit until you die, it is better or worse depending on how long you live. This seems to be the general consensus on what age to file. How long do you think you will be receiving the benefit? In other words, to decide when to file requires you to predict how long you will live in retirement.

What a foolish way to make this important decision. Do you know when you are going to die? Can you base that on family history or your current health? I am reminded of a statement I heard early on in my career, about the best time to buy life insurance – the day before you die. Would it not be nice to know when to buy insurance?

How can you make such an important decision by guessing how long you are going to live? This is one of the biggest mistakes people make in planning for retirement. They are naive about how long they could live. Retirees do not want to contemplate old age. They do not want to consider that they will eventually become frail and need care. The most popular way to decide when to file is by considering how long you will receive benefits. This longevity analysis will help you make the right decision.

People will say their father died at age 72 and they're not going to live that long because their family does not have a long life span. They say they don't want to live to age 90 because their quality of life will be poor. It is as if people think they can end their life to avoid being a burden on someone else. We all know that is not the way it works. Do you know how long you will live? Do you know what medical advances in future years will prolong life? Despite our desire not to grow old, or our denial that we will become frail one day and need help, it will happen.

What you will find with the breakeven analysis is that age 80 is the magic number. If you live past age 80, you should wait to file for Social Security. If you die before age 80, then you should file early. I'm not sure how helpful this is, but people seem to allow this type of analysis to influence at what age they take Social Security benefits. They decide in advance how long they think they will live and then file for benefits based on their expected longevity.

So, what is the optimal/best time to file for Social Security? How do you make that decision? If longevity analysis is not helpful in making the decision, how do you make it? When I teach on the best time to file, I have found the best way to answer that question is with a case study examining a couple looking to retire.

Everyone looking to retire asks the same questions. When can I retire? At what age can I retire? When should I file for Social Security? In answering the general questions that retirees ask, you will see some important principals about when and how to file for Social Security.

Here is the case study I use when teaching seminars on Social Security filing strategies:

When is the best time to file?
Case Study Assumptions

Jim and Sally, age 66

$350,000 of assets for retirement

$3,000 per month budget for retirement needs

At what age can we retire?

Should we file for Social Security at age 66?

Are we at risk to outlive our money?

I want to present to you the example of Jim and Sally. Jim and Sally are both age 66 and looking to retire. There are three assumptions for the case study. The first assumption is that they have $350,000 of assets across all sources, including the house, and their house is paid for. To simplify, I am assuming they have just saved $350,000 during their lifetime to be used for retirement. I am not saying where that money is or reviewing how we favor certain savings or other assets to provide retirement income. Obviously, some assets are more or less favorable to use based on issues like taxes.

The second assumption is that they have a monthly budget of $3,000 for their retirement needs. They don't have any kind of debt, even a mortgage payment, so not much is needed to live.

The assumptions for Jim and Sally are not necessarily important. The important part is to understand the steps necessary to analyze their situation and answer their retirement questions. If you understand how to do the analysis presented here, you can plug in your own numbers and answer the same questions for your individual situation.

The first step in the analysis is to review their budget. I'd want to go over the budget in detail to see how accurate it is and to make sure they put a lot of thought into it. Also, I want to make sure they've considered all of their expenses and have a good idea of the expenses that will and will not continue into retirement. Budgeting is very important in retirement.

Throughout my career, budget discussions have never really been very well received by clients. No one likes to talk about budgets, and people like to do them even less. However, budgets in retirement are even more important than budgets when you're working. When working, if you do not have a budget and overspend, you can make up for it by working additional hours, bonuses, overtime work, or second jobs. You can also refinance your house or consolidate debt. You can do several things while you're working to cover up the overspending. Not so much in retirement. You cannot take another job in retirement. You can't take your bonuses to get caught up. You can no longer make a big commission. Budgeting in retirement is much more important than when working.

For purposes of helping Jim and Sally, a successful retirement analysis depends upon the accuracy of the budget. If the budget is not accurate, then all of the analysis that comes from this will not be very helpful. It will not be a very good predictor of their future and not be very useful to guide retirement decisions. If you are helping someone decide if they can retire, how much they need for retirement income is important. I am amazed people ask me retirement questions but don't really know what they spend or what they will need in retirement.

Advisors love to quote a boilerplate retirement rule of 70%. This means you will need 70% of pre-retirement income for retirement. I disagree with this rule. People spend very differently. Some will need less than 70%, while others will need more. A good budget takes this into account versus blindly following a general rule of thumb.

A lot of people come to me with more than one budget. They will modify it or their spending to accomplish the goal of retirement. They might have one bare-bones budget like the one mentioned in the Jim and Sally example ($3,000/month), with only what they need to pay the bills and get by. They may have another budget that has fun things in it, perhaps travel, grandchildren gifts, or whatever they want to do. They may have a third budget that involves their house. One of the important decisions for people like Jim and Sally is deciding if they want to keep their house or downsize. Would it be better to find another house, maybe a house that's a little bit more manageable with lower maintenance and fewer property taxes that would be more suitable for growing old? A lot of people have raised their kids in their house and have a lot of equity in it. They need to look at the use of that equity for retirement and how helpful it might be. If they stay in the house, they will have limited access to the equity. The needed retirement budget is affected by all of that. The budget will obviously be increased if you have an older home that will need upkeep as you get older. If you cannot meet the higher budget requirements, then you will need to look at downsizing.

I encourage people to have more than one budget because it helps me with the retirement analysis. It helps me give different scenarios to them in order to decide how they want their retirement years to look. It also gives them an objective review of their spending or income needs. I see a lot of spenders change their lifestyles because they are ready to retire, and spending changes are needed to be able to retire.

Can Jim and Sally retire?

Retirement Budget: $36,000	Age 66	Age 70
From Social Security	$22,000	$30,000
From Investments	<14,000>	< 6,000>
Wait until age 70 to file means they will need $36k for 4 years		
Assets to provide income	$350,000	$206,000

Going back to the case study, there are three assumptions for Jim and Sally. The first is $350,000 of assets. The second is a $36,000 yearly budget or $3,000 a month to cover their basic retirement needs. The third is Social Security. For purposes of this example, I provide two different Social Security numbers for comparison and draw conclusions about when to file. The first one assumes that at age 66, which will be their normal retirement age, Jim and Sally would receive $22,000 from Social Security. If they waited till age 70, they could receive $30,000 a year. The difference between the two is the amount by which the Social Security Administration increases the benefit for waiting.

The next step is to subtract that Social Security income number from their budget. This will give them a pretty good indication of whether they have enough assets to retire. If they receive $22,000 a year from Social Security and their budget is $36,000 a year, then they will have to make up the difference, which is $14,000. At age 70, they would need to make up $6,000 a year of additional income from investments to provide for the budget. This illustrates why an accurate budget is so important. Social Security is the largest source of retirement income but most people need additional income. It would be very hard to live on Social Security by itself.

Most will need additional income above Social Security to retire. The planning question for Jim and Sally is $350,000 of assets sufficient to safely produce $14,000 a year of income? Any safe return needs to reflect the current interest rates that can be achieved on investments such as CDs. If a safe return is not possible to produce the income needed, then they need more assets. If the rate of return is not realistic to produce a safe return, then you have your answer— they are not ready to retire, more savings are needed.

Should they draw Social Security at age 66 or draw at age 70? If you were to receive $22,000 at age 66 or $30,000 at age 70, what are the differences between those two choices? If Jim and Sally retire at 66 but do not draw Social Security, they will need to draw down assets until they file at age 70. This will draw down their assets from $350,000 to $206,000 over the four years using the budget of $36,000 per year while waiting to file. At age 70 less income is needed, but they have reduced assets available to produce the additional income necessary.

The next step of analysis would be to determine if they will outlive their assets. The great fear of everyone entering into retirement is the possibility of outliving assets. How do you determine if someone has enough assets to last? A way to figure this out is to divide the available assets by the annual income needed. Again, an accurate retirement budget is needed for this analysis to be useful.

How do you determine if you will outlive your money?

Age 66

$350,000 / $14,000 = 25 years, age 91

Age 70

$206,000 / $6,000 = 34 years, age 104

If Jim and Sally retire at age 66 and then draw Social Security, their assets will last for 25 years, or to age 91. This would make me very uncomfortable because age 91 is not very old. Today's life expectancy for them would be around the middle 80s, which does not leave a lot of margin for the possibility of them living a long life. It is likely they will outlive assets.

Consider if they have an emergency along the way. This analysis is based on a bare-bones budget of $3,000 per month. What if they get sick? What if they have to pay a medical bill? What if the car needs to be repaired or replaced? What if the house needs work? They would have to dip into the $350,000 to cover it. So not running out of money until age 91 is actually a best-case scenario. Any emergencies will reduce the age by which they run out of money. This would make me very nervous, and I would have to conclude that Jim and Sally are not ready to retire. They need more assets and more income to retire successfully.

In contrast, if Jim and Sally retire at age 66 but wait to file for Social Security benefits, their assets last longer. If you divide the two, their multiple is 34. Jim and Sally would not run out of money until age 104. This is almost 20 years past their life expectancy, and there is also some significant margin for emergencies. Surprisingly, their money lasts longer if they wait on Social Security.

So, what is the point of this case study? What am I trying to teach? Here are the important conclusions:

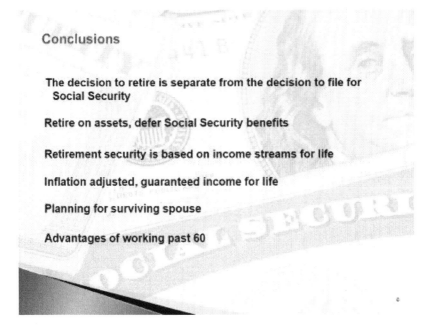

Conclusions

The decision to retire is separate from the decision to file for Social Security

Retire on assets, defer Social Security benefits

Retirement security is based on income streams for life

Inflation adjusted, guaranteed income for life

Planning for surviving spouse

Advantages of working past 60

The first principle is that the decision to retire needs to be made separately from when to file for Social Security. We are conditioned to make these two decisions at the same time. If you are discussing retirement with someone, they will usually mention that they need to go down to the Social Security office and file for their benefits. It is commonly thought these decisions follow each other, but they need to be made independently. Maybe they are the same, maybe not. The case study of Jim and Sally shows they need to be made independently. It was better for them to retire on assets and wait to file.

The second principal is that you should consider retiring on your assets but wait to file for Social Security. This is the most difficult principle for people to understand because it is not logical. Looking at Jim and Sally, most would not decide to spend down their assets while waiting on the increased benefit from Social Security.

Popular logic would be that you work your entire life to accumulate assets, so why would you spend down almost half of your savings over four years just to wait for an increase of $8,000 in Social Security benefits? Isn't the priority to preserve assets? Financial advisors encourage this belief that spending down assets is not wise. Advisors seem to be very reluctant to ever sell assets. They always want to stay invested and emphasize keeping the asset rather than focusing on increasing the income. CPAs think along the same lines and never want to liquidate assets because it usually means there are taxes to be paid. Their thought process is focused only on avoiding taxes.

It does not make sense on the surface by comparing $350,000 of assets, drawn down to $206,000, only to increase Social Security from $22,000 to $30,000.

Why do I advise exchanging almost half of your assets for an $8000 increase in Social Security?

The principle here is that the real value in retirement is the income, not the asset. We focus on the asset while we should be focused on the income. This leads to the third principle of the importance of lifetime income for retirement. "Lifetime income" is income that lasts as long as you last. You cannot outlive it. If Jim and Sally live past age 90 or 100, depending on the scenario, they will be out of assets. But they still will have their Social Security income. This generation has to understand the importance of maximizing lifetime income because of how long we could live in retirement. The possibility that we will live longer in retirement than working should scare us to death! With a long life, Jim and Sally run out of assets but they will always have the lifetime income.

So, when is the optimal time to file for benefits? At what age should you file? What I teach is that everyone should wait until age 70 to file. Whenever I say that, most people think I am saying that they should work until age 70. That is not what I said.

People think the decision to retire is very complex. I disagree. I believe advisors make it complex, which seems to promote the general public's need for retirement advisors. Advisors are valuable, but the retirement question is very simple. I teach everyone they should wait until 70 to file for Social Security. If you want to retire before 70, then you need to have enough assets to draw down while waiting on Social Security. You need to have enough assets after 70 to supplement Social Security and meet any unexpected expenses, such as medical.

Can you retire? The answer is very simple. Everyone should wait until 70, and if you have enough assets to retire before 70, then go for it. But you need to lock in the maximum lifetime income possible from Social Security by waiting. If you do not have enough assets to draw down while waiting, you are not ready to retire. Filing for Social Security early because you need income is not a very good reason to file. If you need money now, where will you be in 20 years?

As a society, how are we doing waiting on Social Security? Today, 75% of retirees file for benefits at age 62. This will irrevocably reduce your payment for life by around 30%. You will collect only 70% of your accrued benefit for the rest of your life. In fact, only 1% of the population waits until age 70 to file. Most people who currently wait until 70 are healthy and working past 70. They wait until 70 because they do not need the money and only file at 70 because their Social Security benefits will not increase past that age.

The key here is how long you will live. Since we do not know the answer to that, when I help clients with retirement planning, I assume everyone is going to live a long life. Obviously, some will live a long life, some will not. It does not matter to me what your genes are or how long your parents lived or what your health situation is. I assume everyone will live a long life because it is the safest and smartest way to help people plan for retirement. If I encourage someone to wait until age 70 to file, and then they pass away at 72, this idea will not help them. You must live past 80 for this idea to be of value. However, I am okay with many not living that long and this recommendation not helping them. My biggest concern for retirees today is living too long. We must protect those that do live past 80 and will be running out of assets. I believe increasing lifetime income by waiting to file is the number one priority. You must be protected for the possibility for living a long life.

Today's retirement planning:

1. Wait until 70 to file to maximize lifetime income

2. A realistic budget for retirement is crucial to planning

3. Determine the additional income needed after maximizing Social Security to cover the budget

4. Determine if you have sufficient assets left to provide the additional income needed safely

5. If you retire before filing, you must have enough assets after drawing down until age 70 and enough assets to cover emergencies after age 70

I describe the Social Security decision as the most important financial decision you will make in your lifetime. Most people would not think of it this way. I believe locking in the most benefit, guaranteed for your lifetime, is the most important financial decision you will make. It is also inflation-adjusted! If we spend as many years in retirement as we do working, inflation will eat us alive. Where else can you find an inflation-adjusted, guaranteed income for life? Income independent of the economy and what is going on in the world because it is guaranteed. That is real security for retirement. Most people would find if they would delay the filing decision to age 70, they would have sufficient income for retirement. Maybe not enough to cover large expenditures, but enough to meet the budget and keep it guaranteed, independent of market investment risk. What an awesome position to be in for retirement, all you income inflation-adjusted and guaranteed. That is what I would call a secure retirement!

Another reason to consider waiting to age 70 is how it will protect our spouses. In the example of Jim and Sally, I assumed they had $22,000 of Social Security. But I did not specify how much was Jim's Social Security benefit and how much was Sally's benefit. Both being age 66, it would be a little unusual for the man to be the same age in a marriage. Usually men are older. And females live longer. Therefore, it is highly likely the women will outlive the men in most marriages. So what?

If Jim died and all the Social Security benefit was his, Sally would refile for his benefit as a widow. Under the Social Security widow rules, married couples are allowed to keep the higher of the two benefits, but not both. Today, benefits are more 50/50 because more working women contributing equally to the household income and retirement benefits. How would Sally feel about a 50% income decrease, if Jim dies? She would only be allowed to keep one benefit, the higher one, and lose the other. Would she have the assets to replace the lost income from losing one Social Security benefit?

It might be surprising to you that the largest segment in poverty in this country, and the fastest growing segment in poverty, are people over the age of 85. Many of them are women and are widows trying to make it on one Social Security benefit. A good number who are in poverty did not start off poor in retirement; they lived too long, someone died, someone got sick and needed expensive care, and they ran out of assets. Now they are living on one Social Security payment, with only limited assets that may be used to create more income.

The best protection for surviving spouses is to maximize the Social Security benefits by waiting until age 70. Not only does it lock in the maximum lifetime income for you for retirement, it also locks in the highest widow benefit for your spouse. Most married couple benefits have at least one significant benefit, and that person should postpone filing. Waiting until age 70 will lock in that benefit for both spouses, to be received as retirement income or survivor benefits.

Retirees entering into the retirement years are usually very comfortable on two benefits, but not prepared to lose one. They don't start out poor, but after medical bills and living too long, they draw down their assets, and they do not have enough to replace the lost income when someone dies. Most retirees do not consider planning for a surviving spouse, and do not realize Social Security's widow rules until it is too late. This is a big reason why I discourage clients from filing for reduced benefits. When you file early, it locks in the widow benefit at that reduced amount. At least one spouse, usually the highest benefit, needs to be maximized by waiting until 70. People in retirement do not usually have life insurance either to protect their spouse. Most drop this because the kids are now grown. We have insurance when the kids are young and need the protection, but most will drop it by retirement because it is too costly. What insurance they have left is usually tied to work and no longer available when they retire. The best way to protect our spouses is by at least maximizing the highest Social Security benefit. This will become the survivor benefit one day. This principal is my response to the objection that you will not live long enough to benefit from delaying filing. The man usually is the one who objects to waiting and states he will not live long enough to justify waiting. My response is that even if that were true, you should still wait because she most likely will live long enough for this idea to benefit her. The widow benefit is the priority. Maybe it will not benefit you but it most likely will benefit her.

One final principle is the importance of *re-calculation.* To understand this, you need to know how your Social Security benefits are calculated. Your benefit is based on the highest 35 years of work income during your lifetime from age 22 to age 60. It is an average of those years with some adjustments for inflation. When you work past age 60, the Social Security office recalculates your benefit if your current income is higher than one of the 35 years. They will replace the lower income year with the higher income and recalculate your benefits. This is significant because most people working past age 60 will be at their highest income during those last years of working. They worked their way up the corporate ladder, and their income is significantly more than at earlier ages. Consider a doctor who has a good income, but that income might not have started until in their mid-30s due to schooling. They may have 10 years of no income counting toward their benefit.

Re-calculation is vital to the retiree because of the increased benefits from it and waiting to file until age 70. Over the decade from ages 60 to 70 you could double your benefit. This is like creating $500k+ in assets for retirement. This is the amount of principal you would need to create the increased amount of inflation-adjusted lifetime income that comes from recalculation and waiting to file for Social Security.

In my practice, about 95% of the clients I help with retirement planning are not prepared for retirement. They are behind. They finally got the kids off their payroll, and they need to catch up. But they will run out of time. They are prepared for a normal retirement but not prepared for something to go wrong, such as someone getting sick or dying.

Most people I see in this situation are doing everything they can to prepare for retirement but will run out of time, and I can only help them so much. Sure, maybe they can change an investment, or I may be able to give them an idea to reduce taxes, but there is only so much I can do to give them more time to save.

I help them understand the importance of lifetime income and the impact of recalculation, the importance of maximizing their Social Security benefits, and helping them understand the benefits of working past age 60. Maximizing lifetime income becomes a priority for the retiree. We must understand the importance of waiting to file. We must face the reality of a long life and the importance of waiting on Social Security. We must not make the decision to file based on an expectation of how long we will live.

Chapter 2 Summary

- **Wait until age 70 to file to maximize lifetime income.**

- **You must know your income needs for retirement. You must have a budget!**

- **Determine the additional income needed after maximizing Social Security to cover the budget.**

- **Determine you have sufficient assets left to provide the additional income needed in retirement, using safe rate of returns. This is after maximizing benefits.**

- **If you retire before filing, you must have enough assets to draw down while waiting, and to provide for emergencies after age 70.**

CHAPTER 3

Secure Retirement

THREE GOALS FOR YOUR ASSETS

Everyone who comes to see me for retirement planning sees the secure retirement handout. Everyone in retirement has the same three goals for their assets. Each of these three categories of assets has very different investment characteristics:

1. Assets needed to provide for spendable income

2. Assets needed to provide for emergencies

3. Assets needed to provide for the long-term, to provide a hedge against inflation, and to provide greater returns that further protect us against inflation

One reason I use this approach is that it provides very clear guidance for what investments should look like to provide the different objectives. Clients often ask me if a certain investment is appropriate. They get annoyed when I answer that it depends. Most investments are not all good or all bad; it depends on the context or goal you are trying to achieve. This is why good advisors spend so much time trying to understand what you want to accomplish.

With a secure retirement, there are three basic goals: spendable assets, emergency assets, and long-term assets. Because of the different objectives, the assets look very different.

SPENDABLE ASSETS

The bucket of spendable assets needs to have investments that are easily accessible and provide guaranteed principal and income. As a result, they're not going to have a very high rate of return. We need these assets to have safety and predictability. We're not looking for high, risky rates of returns; we're looking for safe situations to provide the monthly income we need.

EMERGENCY ASSETS

Assets in the emergency assets bucket need to be accessible in the event of an emergency, such as medical or something happening with the spouse. Because these assets are not as liquid, they will provide a higher rate of return than spendable assets. You also need to control taxation with these assets, which is another characteristic of these types of investments. Controlling taxation will increase the return. Any investment that is there to provide for emergencies needs to contain characteristics of what is listed on the slide above.

LONG-TERM ASSETS

Long-term investments need to provide a higher rate of return to protect against inflation. One of the ways I like to teach about the negative effects of inflation is the following: at 3% inflation, which doesn't seem like much, over 20 years, you lose 50% of your purchasing dollars. That should give you a good idea that we need to be careful about the number of years we spend in retirement, the role that inflation plays in our investments, and our income.

SOME COMMON MISTAKES PEOPLE MAKE IN RETIREMENT

The first mistake is that people tend to be out of balance with respect to the three goals. People tend to have too many assets in one bucket or the other. For example, I usually find a lot of retirees who have all of their assets in the income bucket. In other words, they have all of their assets in the safe bucket, to avoid losses. I understand, but by using this strategy they're not receiving a very high rate of return, which will increase the likelihood of running out of assets. It will also increase the likelihood of income being eroded by inflation.

I also see the other extreme. A lot of people going into retirement have invested their money a certain way their whole life, for growth, but they haven't made the change as they move into retirement. All of their money is in long-term growth investments that are volatile: they're not safe, they're not guaranteed, and this is not the way that I would suggest providing retirement income.

Another mistake I see is people using appropriate assets inappropriately. For example, a lot of people purchase Blue-Chip stocks that pay dividends to provide income. There are a set of stocks of well-known companies that have been around for a long period, some with track records of 50 or 100 years or more. These are very large companies, household names, and thought to be very safe. These companies have very stable dividends and long histories of payments. Are these companies an appropriate way to provide for income? I do not think they are. While the dividend may be stable and predictable, the principal is not. We all know from 2008 what can happen to a Blue-Chip company: it can lose a lot of money. Therefore, I would not use Blue-Chip company stocks to provide income. These are good assets to use for growth, not income, because if you look at the characteristics of spendable assets, one of the characteristics is a guaranteed principal. Investment in a Blue-Chip stock is not guaranteed, and you can absolutely lose money. But is that type of investment inappropriate?

No. I believe that type of investment is the most appropriate investment to provide for long-term growth. I like the predictability of the dividend. I think those household names, those Blue-Chip stocks, are a great way to accumulate growth over a long period. Yes, they will go through ups and downs with the economy. There will be times when they don't look very favorable, and there will be other times when they do look very favorable. But over the long term, I like that type of investment to provide for growth, but I don't like it for income.

Blue-Chip stocks are an example of an asset that is appropriate for most people but used inappropriately. The bucket approach to retirement planning is vital to solidifying your investment objectives, therefore helping you choose suitable investments for each of your goals. When you take the bucket approach, it's hard to be confused by selecting investments that would be inappropriate because clearly, you know exactly what you need to accomplish with your assets. If your asset needs to produce income, then you know exactly what it needs to look like.

If income is the only goal, an asset doesn't need to do anything else. Therefore, it narrows the field of selection of an appropriate investment for that need. At the same time, this will keep you away from other investments that won't be appropriate.

Everybody in retirement has the same three goals: to provide income, to provide for emergencies, and to provide for long-term growth. All three goals are equally important, and you can't choose one over the other. You can't choose to be totally conservative to provide income. You can't choose to put all your money in long-term growth and take that risk. The balanced approach to the bucket retirement planning is the most important goal you can have to help yourself have a secure retirement.

Chapter 3 Summary

- **Everybody in retirement has the same three goals:**
    - **To provide income**
    - **To provide for emergencies**
    - **To provide for long-term growth.**
- **All three goals are equally important, and you can't choose one over the other. You must be balanced.**

CHAPTER 4

Finding Safe Income, Part 1

Over my career, the single biggest change to my practice has been an evolving definition of safe investments. These are things I would have thought of very early on in my career to be safe. However, they turned out not to be so safe in recent years.

One such example is Municipal Bonds. Municipal Bonds are bonds issued by local and municipal governments. Their security is based on the repayment ability of that government. I've always been taught that those types of investments were safe. Well, I happen to live in Jefferson County, Alabama, which has at this time the largest municipal bankruptcy in history. People that bought Jefferson County bonds several years ago have found that those investments were not so safe. They lost their money. Fortunately, those were none of my clients, but a lot of people over the years have purchased Municipal Bonds thinking they were very safe.

Mortgage-backed Securities are also thought of as being very safe. Mortgage-backed Securities are a compilation of mortgages. These types of securities receive the highest credit rating, a Triple "A" rating by the bond agencies. A credit rating of Triple "A" is usually reserved for the safest asset. And yet, despite that, we found that you can lose significant money by investing in Mortgage-backed Securities. In fact, Mortgages and Mortgage-backed Securities just about brought down the entire economy in 2008.

Over my lifetime, I never would have thought that banks were not safe. I would have never envisioned a time when banks went out of business at the rate they've gone out of business in recent years. I would never have thought that the FDIC would have to be so involved in bailing out banks. In fact, during 2008–2010, I was very concerned that the FDIC was going to run out of money and need a bailout from the public. So many banks were going under that the FDIC insurance kicked in at a rate I had never seen before.

People talk about Blue-Chip companies being safe. Blue-Chip is a generic term that a lot of people give to very safe companies, household names such as Coca-Cola. These Blue-Chip companies have been around forever. Are these companies safe? When you say the words "Blue-Chip", it certainly sounds like it, but as we learned in 2008, that's not quite the case. Those companies can lose a lot of money regardless of how long they've been around and how much of a household name they are.

What investments should you consider to safely provide income? The first step to understanding the answer is to make sure you *maximize the guaranteed sources of income available to you.* The two guaranteed sources of income that we have in life are Social Security and pensions. Not everybody has a pension, but for those who do, there are some things which I want to talk about a little later. Maximizing your Social Security benefit ought to be the most important thing you do because Social Security is the largest source of guaranteed income most people have during their lifetime in retirement.

That's why the decision of when and how you receive your Social Security benefit is such an important retirement decision. It is the most important retirement decision you will make in your lifetime. When you successfully maximize your Social Security benefit, you create a situation in which more of your income is now guaranteed, and in which more of your income will increase in the future due to cost of living increases. Therefore, future income is less influenced by inflation and other negative factors in the economy. The more guaranteed your income, the less your future income will be affected by inflation and other economic factors such as a down economy. The more guaranteed your income, the less you are reliant upon non-guaranteed income, which comes from investments.

I encourage retirees to wait until age 70 to file for Social Security. In the example that I gave previously about Jim and Sally, they had two choices: they could receive Social Security at age 66, or they could take it at age 70. If they took Social Security at age 66, they would need to provide an additional $14,000 from their investment income. If they wait until age 70, they only have to provide $6,000 of additional income. The higher the guaranteed amount of your income, the less dependent you are on the non-guaranteed investment income. Therefore, this will help garner a more secure retirement. This is particularly important in periods of low interest rates when safe returns are hard to find.

In the example of Jim and Sally, I mention that Jim and Sally would have $205,000 of assets at age 70 instead of $350,000 at age 66. Those assets would need to produce $6,000 of income in addition to Social Security to make their budget. The point is that by waiting until age 70 and locking in the higher Social

Security amount, their assets are reduced but they need to produce less income. This is a safer avenue in retirement because more of your income is guaranteed. You will be less dependent upon investment income.

At age 70, Jim and Sally will have $206,000 of assets left to create $6000 of income. It is not going to take $206,000 to produce $6,000 a year of income. In fact, it's only going to take about $100,000 of assets to produce $6,000 a year of income. Therefore, the rest of their assets, the $106,000 extra, could then be used for the other buckets, such as emergency funds or long-term growth.

This is only possible if you don't need to use all of your assets to provide income. If you raise your guaranteed income through Social Security and reduce the non-guaranteed component of investment income, then you will have the option of having different investment objectives with your different assets.

Your priority is to maximize the lifetime income available from Social Security. This comes from waiting until age 70, recalculation of benefits, and using the proper filing strategy depending upon your specific situation. The increase of lifetime income secured from waiting to file Social Security benefits is so valuable, especially when you consider the limited ways to produce safe income.

For some reason, the public does not seem to value the increase in benefits. The Social Security is raising your benefit 8% for every year past FRA (Full Retirement Age) that you wait to file. If I could guarantee a no risk, 8%, tax-free rate of return, would you take it? Of course you would! Well, the government is giving that to you, but for some reason most people don't take it. If it is more challenging to find a safe income investment, why would you not just take the 8% return given to you by the government?

Chapter 4 Summary

- To provide safe income, your first goal should be to maximize the guaranteed sources of income available to you, namely pensions and Social Security.

- In order to maximize Social Security, you also need to know the proper filing strategy, which depends upon your specific situation (see next chapters).

CHAPTER 5

Filing Strategies For Married and Divorced Couples

There are two specific strategies for maximizing your Social Security benefit for married couples. Both of these strategies depend upon your ability to understand the spousal benefit. Spousal benefits are the most misunderstood Social Security filing strategy. More people leave money on the table with spousal benefits more than with any other strategy. A big reason for this is that the spousal benefit is never mentioned on your earnings and benefit statement.

The common mistake is that when you receive an earnings statement from the Social Security Administration telling you what your benefit is, it doesn't have any mention whatsoever of a spousal benefit. People assume filing for their own benefit is their only way to file. The spousal benefit has nothing to do with your work history or how much Social Security taxes you paid, in your lifetime. What makes you eligible for the benefit and who benefits from the spousal benefit?

Filing Strategies for married couples

Spousal Benefit Requirements
- Age 62
- 1 year or more of marriage
- Spouse must be collecting a benefit
- Benefit = 50% Spouse's retirement benefit at full retirement age

The spousal benefit is a benefit that's available at age 62 or older to couples who have been married at least one year, which applies to most married couples in this country. The spousal benefit is equal to 50% of your spouse's full retirement benefit. The full retirement benefit, or FRA, is what someone will receive at their normal retirement age. This is determined by your date of birth. If you are not certain, you can find it on the Social Security's website (ssa.gov).

If your spouse will receive $3,000 a month at FRA, you would be eligible for 50% of that, or $1,500. Note that if your spouse took their benefit early, it affects *their* benefit but does not reduce your spousal benefit. Also, if your spouse took their benefit late, such as at age 70, you do not benefit from the increase for the spousal benefit. It is still based on FRA. This is why you will find waiting until age 70 is a great idea for your own benefit, but it does not make a difference in a spousal benefit. There is never a reason to wait to file for it beyond your FRA. The 8% increases to benefits only apply to your own benefit and not the spousal benefit (and divorced benefit, later discussed).

Two groups are helped by the spousal benefit: a spouse (usually a woman) who stayed home with children and had limited compensation; or a spouse who worked in a profession with a low-income history. In those situations, even though the Social Security Administration sends you an earnings statement saying what your benefit is based on your earning and taxes paid, you ignore it, and you never file for it. Instead you file for the spousal benefit because it is higher.

The spousal benefit is entirely driven by your spouse's benefit at FRA and the income they made during their career. Even if you have never worked or paid Social Security taxes, this is true and you can still receive a spousal benefit. You file for 50% of your spouse's benefit because it is higher than your own benefit. Traditionally, this strategy benefits women.

The key to the spousal benefit is that, to receive it, one spouse must be collecting a benefit for the other one to be eligible for filing for a spousal benefit. Spousal benefits are not available unless at least one spouse is collecting a benefit. You cannot just file for it. If a husband is collecting a benefit, then the wife is eligible for a spousal benefit. If the wife is collecting a benefit, then the husband will be eligible for a spousal benefit off her benefit. The spousal benefit may or may not be better than filing for your own benefit, but you are eligible to file for it only if your spouse is receiving a benefit.

In 2015, the Social Security claiming rules changed significantly. Until that time, we could pick and choose benefits, and we were given a lot of leeway in how we could file. After 2015, there were new restrictions put in place because lawmakers felt there was considerable abuse with Social Security filing. Many of the ways people were taking advantage of the Social Security system and the filing strategies were never really intended.

In 2015, a system we call "deemed filing" was implemented. When you file for Social Security, you're deemed to be filing for *all* available Social Security, whether you want those benefits or not, and whether you are receiving those benefits or not. We don't really have the option of filing certain ways and coming back and changing them later. Once you file, that's pretty much it. If you are eligible for more than one Social Security benefit, you will receive the higher of the two under the new deemed filing rules. You cannot pick and choose which benefit you would like to receive.

Three exceptions have been put in place to the deemed filing rules. We will cover the other two in later chapters. The first exception is for married couples. If you qualify for the spousal benefit, and you were born before 1954, you may file what is called a restricted application. A restricted application tells the Social Security office that you want to restrict your benefit. Remember, under the new rules you will automatically receive the higher of any benefits for which you are eligible. When you are eligible for the spousal benefit, you also will be eligible for your own benefit. The restricted application tells the Social Security office which benefit you want to receive. You might be thinking, why would you not want the higher benefit? Why would you want to choose or restrict a benefit?

This is why. If you were born before 1954 you can file for a spousal benefit while still filing for your own benefit later. Even though you file for a spousal benefit, you will not freeze your own benefit, which will continue to increase by 8% per year. Your own benefit continues to increase and you could file twice for the increased amount at age 70. Under the restricted application, you restrict your benefit to the spousal benefit only while waiting on your own benefit until age 70. Under the new rules, you will receive the higher of the two benefits. In this case, you are filing for the lower spousal benefit while waiting on your own benefit.

If you were born after 1954, you do not have that ability. Once you file, that's it. Restricted application for the spousal benefit is a very specific filing strategy with the Social Security Administration, telling them you only want the spousal benefit even though you qualify for your own benefit. Remember you qualify for both benefits but restrict it to the spousal benefit only while waiting on your own benefit to age 70. If those born after 1954 were to file for a spousal benefit and come back at age 70, they would find their benefit had not gone up by the delayed retirement credits. It was frozen because of the deemed filing rules. Once you file, you cannot collect a benefit by itself. You can't restrict receipt of your benefits under the new rules. The Social Security office would force you to file for the higher benefit, which is you own benefit. Therefore you would never receive the 8% increases from waiting to file.

The first group that benefits from the spousal benefit is the lower income benefit spouses. They can file for 50% of their spouse's benefit because it is higher than their own benefit. For that person, they will not ever file for their own benefit because 50% of their spouses benefit is always going to be greater than their own benefit. Typically, this is for women who lack work history because they have been home with children.

The second group that benefits from the spousal benefit is the higher earning spouses using the 1954 exception. You may file for one half of your spouse's benefit while later filing for your own benefit. Because you are eligible for more than one benefit, you must restrict the benefit. You tell the Social Security office you only want the spousal benefit, and will file for your own benefit later. Remember, your own benefit is greater and will automatically be filed for, and if that happens you will not receive the 8% increase. Restricting the benefit to the spousal benefit only allows you to receive the 8% and later file for your own benefit. I see this all the time where one spouse is already receiving their benefit while the other is working and planning to file at age 70. Often this is the woman, and they file for their benefit early at age 62 because it is not much. The higher income spouse could receive one half right now without messing up the plan to file at 70. This could be saved and put in the bank right now!

It is important to note that for eligibility for the spousal benefit, a spouse must be collecting *a* benefit. That benefit is not necessarily a retirement benefit. Disability will qualify you. If one spouse is receiving disability while the other is still working, the spouse that is still working qualifies for a spousal benefit. They could file for the spousal benefit (one half of the disability), and then come back and file for their own benefit when they reach 70. They could switch to their own benefit, filing twice – once for the spousal and once for their own benefit – if they were born before 1954.

With the Restricted Application, when you file you do not take your own benefit, even though you may be eligible. You instead collect a spousal benefit while deferring your own benefit. You then switch to your own benefit later because it's higher. This is the born-before-1954 strategy. If you turned 62 by December 31, 2015, you're eligible for this exception. If you did not turn age 62 by 12/31/2015, you are not eligible, because once you file, you are under the new rules.

It is important to note that you have a do-over strategy with Social Security. A filing decision within the first twelve months may be reversed. If any information in this book has caused you to rethink your strategy for filing for Social Security and you want to refile, you are allowed a do-over, if the initial filing took place in the last 12 months.

If you have filed for Social Security early, and I have convinced you to wait, you can go back within one year, undo that decision, and let your benefit go back to increasing to age 70. You do have to pay back the benefits. There's no penalty, there's no interest associated with that, and you are only allowed to do this if you change your mind within twelve months of the initial filing. After twelve months, you are not able to reverse it.

Often, I find the lower benefit spouse will file for their benefit early or at FRA, while the other spouse is still working. At that time, the person filing for their own benefit will not be eligible for the higher spousal benefit because their spouse is not collecting a benefit. They miss the opportunity to file later for the higher spousal benefit amount because they do not recognize they are now eligible. When the initial filing was done, they were not eligible for the spousal benefit, but will become eligible at a later date. No one ever tells them they need to refile when eligible.

The second most common mistake people make when filing for Social Security is with the divorced benefits. This is not quite as common a mistake as with a spousal benefit, but I do find that a lot of people do not know they are eligible to receive a divorced benefit, and do not know how to determine if it will help them.

Planning Strategy: Divorced Benefits

- Single, age 62+
- Spouse may be dead or alive
- Married for 10 years)

- No deemed filing if you wait until full retirement age

What makes you eligible for a divorced benefit? To be eligible for a divorced benefit, you have to be single, aged 62 or older, and to have been married for ten years or more. Like the spousal benefit, you are filing on the earnings record of another because you will receive more benefit than you own benefit. The difference is that in this case, you are filing on an ex-spouse. The divorced benefit is mainly a help to those who do not have a significant benefit based on their own work history. Again, this is usually a situation where someone has a low-income history and does not have a large benefit because they've been home with children. They're better off filing for

50% of their ex-spouse's benefit rather than their own benefit because the ex-spouse's benefit is higher. In contrast, the spousal benefit is 50% of your current spouse's FRA, not the ex.

Divorced benefits are often overlooked because, just like spousal benefits, they are not on your earnings statement. There's no mention of them. You must just know that you qualify for it. If you're remarried, you're not eligible for a divorced benefit. If you were married only 9 years, you are not eligible – the eligibility is pretty black and white – 10 years of marriage and single.

There is one exception to being remarried. In general, you will lose divorced benefits if you remarry. However, this is not the case if you are receiving benefits as a divorced spouse, and if you marry someone receiving benefits on someone else's record, you can continue to receive benefits on you prior spouses' record. There are also exceptions to the requirement 10 years of marriage, relative to having a child. This is beyond the scope of this book. I just want to mention, if you have not been married for ten years, you might still qualify for a divorced benefit.

Some are concerned about eligibility for the benefit because of what is happening with the ex-spouse. In general, it doesn't matter what was going on with the ex-husband or the ex-wife. It does not matter whether or not they are receiving their Social Security. It does not matter if the ex is not at retirement age or is not working. When you file for the divorced benefit, if it has been less than two years since the divorce was initially filed, there are complications. Both parties do need to be age 62, which will affect you if a spouse is several years younger. If it is more than two years from when the divorce was initially filed, there are no complications. It is a legal benefit for you, take it if helpful. If you have more than one ex, and you qualify for the ten years for each, you can pick the higher of the two. You can pick whichever ex-spouse produced a higher benefit and file for that.

Some of the most common questions I receive about divorced benefits are whether the ex will be notified and whether it's going to have any kind of effect on their retirement. Usually, when someone asks me that, it's a situation where there's a lot of tension, and they don't want to do anything that will create problems. Your ex is not notified. It's not going to have any effect on their benefit. This is a divorced benefit to which you're legally entitled if you're single, age 62, and were married to them for 10 years or more.

The biggest planning issue most people have with divorced benefits is verifying the divorced benefit because it's based on the records of another person. Most of the time in a divorce situation, someone may not know what kind of benefit exists because they don't know what the income history has been for the ex. A lot of times during the divorce, one spouse may have been hiding income, or there may have been other issues. Often, an ex-husband doesn't want you to know what their income is. The Social Security Administration also sees this as a privacy issue because it's based on the Social Security number of another person, and they don't freely give this information.

For planning purposes, and to take advantage of the divorced benefit (if 50% of your ex-spouse's benefit is greater than yours), you can call the Social Security office and make an in-person appointment. You cannot do this over the phone, and you cannot do this over the Internet. You must make an appointment, take your divorce decree and your marriage certificate, and go there in person. You must prove you were married to that person for 10 years or more, and that you are eligible for the divorced benefit. This is the only way you can verify the benefit.

Once you verify that benefit, you may find your own benefit is greater than 50% of you ex's benefit, in which case you don't ever want to file for a divorced benefit. But you are not going to know that until you verify it. Usually, when I'm working with someone who is divorced, they have returned to work to rebuild their finances and have a benefit. In this case we don't know if the divorced benefit is higher and will help. I just want them to get the information, and then we can look at which way is the best way to file.

There are two divorced benefits: One if the divorced spouse is alive, and one if the divorced spouse is deceased. Divorced widow benefits will be covered in the next chapter. If the ex-spouse is living, the benefit is equal to 50% of their full retirement age benefit or FRA.

The second exception to the deemed filing rules is with divorced benefits. If you were born before 1954, and you wait until full retirement age to file for a divorced benefit, you have a deemed filing exception. This means you can come back and file for your own benefit at age 70. This strategy is very similar to the one we use for the spousal benefits, where you may receive the spousal benefit and yet come back later and file for your own benefit at age 70.

This is also a restricted application strategy, just like the spousal benefit. With the previous exception, you were filing for a restricted application for spousal benefits only, and now you are filing for a restricted application for divorced benefits only. The same logic applies because you qualify for more than one benefit and need to restrict which one you receive.

You file for a divorce benefit at your full retirement age, receive that for several years, and then come back and file for your own benefit amount at age 70. That deemed filing exception only exists if you were born before 1954 and you wait until full retirement age to file for the divorced benefit. If you don't qualify under those exceptions, you won't be able to file twice. Also, you can't file for a divorced benefit before your full retirement age, even if you were born before 1954. You could have filed early for spousal benefits under this exception, but not for divorced benefits. It must be FRA.

In closing this chapter, I want to point out a common mistake with spousal benefits. The scenario is when a one person of a married couple has a significant benefit and the other, usually the woman, has a much smaller benefit. Often the smaller benefit is filed for early while waiting on the larger spousal benefit.

The thought process is that taking a 30% discount on a small benefit is not such a big deal. It is assumed that the much larger spousal benefit will be there later, and received for most of one's retirement years. So once your spouse files and you become eligible for the spousal benefit, you switch.

Under the deemed filing rules, when the spousal benefits are filed for later they will be reduced, even though the later spousal benefits were not filed for early. Often, couples will file for the smaller benefit thinking the reduction from filing early will not affect the eventual spousal benefit. Surprise – it does. The spousal benefit, even though it was not filed for early, will be considered early and subsequently reduced. This comes as a shock for retirees. This does not happen with divorced benefits using the restricted application because you cannot file early and still be eligible for the exception. The examples above are just a few more reasons why I strongly discourage anyone from filing for any benefits before the FRA.

Chapter 5 Summary

- The first group that benefits from the spousal benefit is the lower income benefit spouses. They can file for 50% of their spouse's benefit because it is higher than their own benefit.

- The second group that benefits is the higher earning spouses, using the 1954 exception. You may file for one half of your spouse's benefit, while later filing for your own benefit.

- Like the spousal benefit, with the divorced benefit you are filing on the earnings record of another because you will receive more benefit. The difference is that in this case, you are filing on an ex-spouse.

- If you were born before 1954, and you wait until full retirement age to file for a divorced benefit, you have a deemed filing exception. This means that you can come back and file for your own benefit at age 70.

CHAPTER 6

Widow And Divorced Widow Benefits

The third situation in which many mistakes are made is with widow benefits. Most people are aware of the widow benefit. Unlike other benefits, such as spousal or divorced, widow benefits are mentioned on your earning statement.

To qualify for a widow benefit, a person must have been married for nine months or more, although there are exceptions, such as if the spouse died in an accident or was killed while serving in the military. In those situations, if a person has not been married for nine months or more, they might still qualify for a widow benefit. But in general, widow benefits are available to people who have been married for nine months or more.

The widow benefit is equal to 100% of the full retirement age (FRA) benefit the deceased would have received at FRA, or is receiving at the time they are deceased. This is another reason why I encourage people to wait until age 70 to file. If someone receives Social Security early and it's reduced, the widow benefit will also be reduced.

The biggest area of confusion for widow benefits concerns what happens when you remarry. In a divorce situation, if you're single, you're eligible for the divorced benefit, but if you remarry, you're not. In a widow's situation, you can still qualify for a widow benefit if you remarry after age 60. If you remarry before age 60, you will not be eligible for a widow benefit. If you remarry after 60, you have a choice in how you want to file. You might want to file for the widow benefit, or you might want to file for a spousal benefit with your new husband or wife. You might want to file for your own benefit.

Deciding which way to file comes down to earnings history. Here's an easy way to think about it: If you were married to a brain surgeon and he or she died, you may then remarry a teacher. In this case, you will probably want to file for the widow benefit. If you were married to a teacher and he or she died and you remarry a brain surgeon, you will probably want to file for the spousal benefits. Benefits come down to income history of your current spouse versus the deceased.

The third of the three exceptions to the deemed filing rules is for the widow benefit. As you may recall, the first exception is for married couples. To review: If you are eligible for a spousal benefit and you were born before 1954, you have the option of filing for a spousal benefit *only*, and then reserving the right to come back and file for your own benefit at age 70. That exception exists for a divorced benefit if you were born before 1954 and you wait until your own full retirement age.

The third exception to the deemed filing rules is for the widow benefit. With a widow benefit, you can receive a benefit as early as age 60, yet still come back and file for your own benefit later. You can file for a widow benefit and then switch to your own benefit later at age 70. There's no requirement that you be born before 1954, or that you file for the widow benefit at or after full retirement age. Those two requirements are not needed for the deemed filing exception for widow benefits. If you're eligible for a widow benefit, then you always have the option of filing for it as early as age 60 by itself as a restricted application, while still coming back and filing for your own benefit at age 70.

Because widow benefits always have a deemed filing exception, filing early will not reduce the later filing. You may recall that if you file for spousal benefits early, you will be considered to be filing for later benefits early as well. Even though the second filing was not early, it will be considered early and reduced also. This is not true for widow benefits.

Planning Strategy: Widow Benefit

- 9+ months
- Not remarried unless after 60
- Remarried after 60, file on new spouse
- Length of marriage exception
- No deemed filing for survivor benefits

SOCIAL SECURITY®

In addition to married couples, divorced couples also have a widow benefit. The difference is that the benefit is based on the ex-spouse's FRA. If you qualify for divorced benefits and the ex passes away, you are now entitled to a divorced widow benefit, which doubles the benefit. A normal divorced benefit is 50% of FRA, while a widow benefit is 100% of FRA.

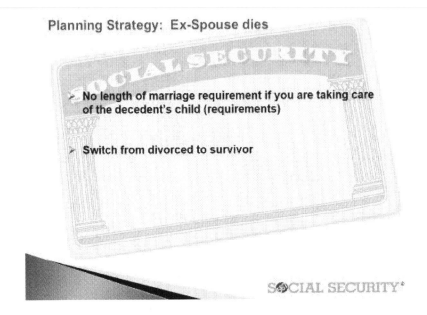

Planning Strategy: Ex-Spouse dies

➢ No length of marriage requirement if you are taking care of the decedent's child (requirements)

➢ Switch from divorced to survivor

SOCIAL SECURITY*

If your ex-spouse has passed away, you qualify for divorced widow benefits if:

- Marriage lasted for 10 years

- You are age 60 or older

- You are single or re-married after age 60

The most common filing error I see with divorced benefits is not realizing the impact of the divorced widow benefit. Quite often, someone verifies the 50% divorced benefit and realizes it will not help them. This is because their own benefit is greater than 50% of their ex-spouse's benefit. Remember, the ex-spouse's benefit doubles if the ex passes away. The 50% benefit will not help them but the 100% will help them. Quite often, because they have returned to work and have some work history, 50% is not a benefit, but 100% is definitely a benefit. No one tells them to refile for the widow benefit. You just have to know if it is better than your own benefit or the normal divorce benefit.

Chapter 6 Summary

- **You can receive a widow benefit as early as age 60, yet still come back and file for your own benefit later.**

- **Remember, the divorced benefit may not help you initially, but the divorced widow benefit most likely will.**

CHAPTER 7

Finding Safe Income, Part 2

Over the years, the biggest change in my practice has been the evolving definition of the word "safety." A lot of things that were always thought of as being safe have turned out not to be so safe. 2008 opened our eyes to a lot of unforeseen risk, for instance, the safety of bonds.

I was always taught that Municipal Bonds were safe. These bonds are IOUs issued by municipalities, backed by the full faith of the issuing municipality and their ability to pay their obligation. I was taught Municipal Bonds were very safe. It was backed by the municipality's ability to pay their bills. I was taught municipal bonds are great ways to generate income. As it turns out, that's not so true.

Another lesson of 2008 was that mortgages were not so safe. This was true even though mortgages used to receive the highest credit rating possible. People thought of real estate as being a very safe, very consistent, and conservative investment. Most people never considered that real estate would go down in value. We learned, however, that mortgages are quite risky and real estate can go down in value.

The mortgage and real estate world brought down the entire economy in 2008-2009.

For my whole life, I have always thought of banks as being very safe places for your savings. Who would have ever thought we would have gone through a period when banks were going under right and left? Who would have ever thought we would have gone through a period of so many bail-outs by the federal government through the FDIC?

Another big lesson we learned in 2008 was that there is a big conflict of interest between bond rating agencies and their bond ratings. Rating agencies of bonds determined the safety of a particular bond by rating the issuer of the bond. Many rating agencies determined certain types of bonds to be very safe and of the highest possible quality. Not true!

Further, we learned there's a huge conflict of interest because the people who pay for the ratings are the bond issuers. So, it's in their best interest to receive a high rating and to be viewed as a safe bond. The rating agencies are obliged to provide those ratings and to keep the money coming in for the research, which turned out to be a huge conflict of interest.

Is there anything safe anymore? Is there anything I can recommend to clients for retirement income and still call it safe? Answering that question has been the single biggest advice change to my practice. I really wrestled with the lessons of 2008. The definition of a safe income investment is very different today than what it was a decade ago.

Top priority for retirees is to make sure their guaranteed income is maximized. This is why the Social Security decision is so important. Social Security is the largest source of guaranteed income that we have for life. All retirees need to make sure that before they start receiving Social Security, they are applying for the best possible way to increase their benefits. So, step one in retirement planning is to maximize your Social Security benefit. What could be safer than maximizing your guaranteed income?

Step two would be to maximize other sources of guaranteed income. One example of that would be a pension. Many people do not have a pension, but a lot of people still do. How can you maximize your pensions? A pension, just like Social Security, is a guaranteed stream of income for your life. The most common mistake that I see with people who receive pensions is the decision of how they want to receive the pension. Most people understand that before you start pension payments you have to choose how you want to receive them. There are different possibilities. You can receive payments based on your life. You can also receive payments based on your life and then have a survivorship option for a spouse, as well as other options.

Each of those different options has different amounts associated with them. What is the best way to receive income? There is no general rule or answer for that question, but the mistake most people make is not considering all the possibilities. You might find that a pension payment on your life is the best option. This is going to happen in a lot of cases where the difference between the survivorship options and the single life option are very different. The planning solution is to understand why that difference exists.

For example, let's say you have a choice between two pension options: one that pays $4,000 on your life or one that pays $3,000 on your life and the $3,000 payment continues to be paid to your spouse if something happens to you. What is the difference between the $4,000 on your life and the $3,000 on your life with a survivorship option? That extra $1,000 is for life insurance purchased through your pension plan. In general, that's not really a good idea. I've seen pension plans where that was a very attractive option. I've seen plans where it was not. In your pension planning, you must consider how much life insurance would be necessary to duplicate the continuation of the income, and what the cost would be.

If you have a $1,000 difference between the two payments, can you buy enough insurance with that $1,000 to continue the $3,000 a month? In many cases you can. If so, you would take the higher pension amount, and then take some of that increased difference to buy life insurance to protect your spouse, and pocket the difference.

It might only take $500 to buy life insurance that would duplicate the survivorship option of your pension. You can then buy life insurance for $500 a month that will continue a stream of income of $3,000 for your spouse, and pocket the other $500 for the rest of your life.

There are several factors involved here, including the pension plan itself, the payment amount difference between the options, the cost of insurance to duplicate the survivorship options, and your health. Can you obtain insurance? Will that insurance have a good rating? Do you have health situations that would cause an increase in the cost of said insurance? Your health situation might mean that you're better off choosing the survivorship option with your pension plans. But, if you're healthy, you're probably going to find that you are better off with the competitive insurance market. Obtain help from an insurance agent to determine all your options, rather than just automatically taking survivorship options with your pension plan. You might find it's better or you might find that it's not.

Once you have the maximum amount of Social Security and the maximum amount of your pensions available to you, then you can look at other ways to create your retirement income. In the bucket approach that we talked about in previous chapters, one of the asset categories was spendable assets. In that category, I discussed assets that were set aside to produce spendable income. Some characteristics of this type of asset is that the money needs to be easily accessible, the principal needs to be guaranteed, and you should not have any risks or fluctuations associated with that money. Because of the assets being liquid and guaranteed, you're not going to receive a very high rate of return either.

What are some examples today of things that would generate safe, predictable income? My favorite way to generate safe, predictable income is through an Immediate Annuity. Usually, when I bring up the word "annuity," it's met with resistance because of the belief that annuities are not very favorable investments. The types of annuities that usually garner that response are Variable Annuities, and I would agree with that.

But an Immediate Annuity is a different type of annuity. In this chapter, you'll learn about two types of annuities that I believe are very appropriate. I do believe that Immediate Annuities are a great way to provide safe income for retirees. Remember the importance of Lifetime Income – that means having sources of income that extend for your lifetime. This type of asset is like having an infinite asset, one without end, because it is always there providing income. We don't know how long we are going to live in retirement, so we want sources of income that will last our lifetime, whether we live to be 80, 90, 100, or 110 years old. We need to have sources of income that we cannot outlive. If we don't, we may outlive our assets, but we will not outlive lifetime income.

I recommend Immediate Annuities to provide safe lifetime income. An Immediate Annuity is where you exchange a lump sum for an income. You might go to an insurance company and exchange $150,000 for $1,500 per month for life. I like to describe an Immediate Annuity as having your own private pension for life.

Social Security, pensions, and Immediate Annuities are the three different ways you can guarantee an income for your lifetime. Here are the key steps:

- Maximizing Social Security is step one.

- Maximizing your pension, if you have one, is step two.

- Securing an Immediate Annuity is step three.

Many people who don't have pensions will want to look at Immediate Annuities as a way to supplement their Social Security. If you have a pension, you probably don't need an Immediate Annuity because you will already have 2 sources of guaranteed income for life.

I first started looking at Immediate Annuities when I tried to find safe substitutes for bonds; I wanted to find an alternative to avoid their default risk and interest rate risk. Bonds carry default risks and interest rates risk which are misunderstood by the public: when rates are rising, bonds lose money. Therefore, increasing interest rates are not very favorable for bonds. We already discussed the possible default risk of bonds. The possibility the issuer will not be able to repay the IOU.

I believe Immediate Annuities are a great substitute for bonds, and are safer. They generally provide higher returns than Treasury Bonds, with similar safety. Immediate Annuities are also the only way to create income for life outside of a pension or Social Security. Immediate Annuities work much like a bond. The risk associated with them is the risk of the issuer to fulfill the obligation. A bond is a future IOU. It is as if you are loaning money to a company, municipality, or government, and the bond is a promise of repayment at a future date. In the meantime, they're going to pay you interest. The IOU is reflective of current interest rates and the entity's ability to repay at a future date. A Treasury Bond is an IOU of the government, which is why it is considered to be so safe.

Bonds are influenced by current interest rates such as when interest rates go up, bond IOU is devalued. A bond's rate of return is determined at the time of purchase, and reflects interest rates at that time. Therefore, if rates increase, the bond becomes less valuable because you could duplicate the same arrangement at the higher current rate.

The risk associated with all bonds is whether the entity will be able to repay the money at a future date. In the situation of a Treasury Bond, for example, the reason it receives the highest possible safety rating is that the IOU is backed by the full faith and credit of our government. It's backed by our government's ability to repay its bills.

Municipal Bonds are backed by the ability of municipal governments to pay their bills. As it turns out, municipal governments have had some difficulty repaying their bonds, so a lot of people have lost money with bonds. In the same way, the risk of the Immediate Annuity is the insurance company's ability to honor the income stream. If you swapped $150,000 to an insurance company on a promise that they pay you $1,500 of income for the rest your life, then the strength and the security of that insurance company matters. So, the risk associated with an Immediate Annuity is going to be the insurance company's financial strength. It is important to note the additional layer of safety which exists from a back-up guarantee for insurance companies, similar to the banks with the FDIC.

I recommend Immediate Annuities over bonds because of their safety. They are provided by insurance companies and I believe insurance companies are the safest of all financial institutions. They showed this to me in 2008. This obligation of an Immediate Annuity is an asset of the insurance company. In the example of $150,000 for $1,500 of income for life, the income obligation is backed by the strength of the insurance company. They try to produce a rate of return greater than what they're paying you for the income. I like the safety of insurance companies, particularly over banks. I like that insurance companies are highly regulated and less likely to get into riskier investments, like mortgages, which got the banks into trouble.

Since 2008, regulations have been put in place to try to prevent another crisis, but those types of regulations have existed for insurance companies for years. I like that we have several independent rating agencies for insurance companies. This decreases the likelihood of compromised ratings. Bonds have had essentially one rating agency: Moody's. When we hear about AAA ratings, that's what we are talking about. Insurance companies are rated by multiple agencies. There are five major agencies that have been around for my entire career. The information associated with the strength and security of the insurance company, I believe, is more readily available than what exists for banks, or even for companies and municipalities that provide bonds. It is just easy to get an idea of their safety.

Consumers need to pay attention to the financial security and strength of the company providing the Immediate Annuity. You can't just go with the highest payment of income. You must find a balance between safety of the company and being competitive with other insurance companies.

Some insurance companies that I recommend for clients have been around for 100 to 150 to even 200 years. That is an amazing record when you think about everything that has happened in the world in the past 200 years. From wars to the Great Depression, and much more, these insurance companies have stood the test of time. That is why I favor them as the most appropriate way to provide safe income, especially in comparison to CDs, banks, real estate, corporate bonds, municipal bonds, or other ways to provide income.

I like Immediate Annuities because their rate of return is generally greater than that of Treasury Bonds. I don't believe you will give up anything from a safety standpoint. I think the additional risk associated with the insurance company is well worth it. So, when you're shopping for Immediate Annuities, make sure you're paying full attention to the safety and security of the insurance company. You need to dig a little deeper and see what the financial situation is from the information available from the different rating agencies.

I also recommend that you diversify your lump sums. If you have a $150,000 lump sum that you want to convert to an Immediate Annuity, perhaps you could do that with two or three different companies. It doesn't have to be one company. That way all your income is not dependent upon the future of one insurance company.

One of the questions I receive from time to time concerns what I think about the Variable Annuities that have guaranteed income riders. Quite often, brokers and advisers will push Variable Annuities with guaranteed income riders. The thought process is that your money is very safe, even though it's invested in the stock market. A Variable Annuity with a guaranteed income rider is not a substitute for guaranteed income, at least not in the way of the Immediate Annuities I am speaking of. I know a lot of people think it is, but it is not, and should not be sold that way.

Next to Immediate Annuities, I like providing income with the Reverse Mortgage. The Reverse Mortgage is the most misunderstood financial product in the world. I find very few people who truly understand how it can be used, and what advantage it has.

Just like any other financial product, Reverse Mortgage will fit some people, but it's not for everyone. Certain situations will determine whether it is a good idea or not. I just want people to consider Reverse Mortgage as a possible source of safe income. A lot of people don't even consider it because they read somewhere or heard somewhere that it's not a good deal.

The main way I use a Reverse Mortgage is to reduce the retirement budget by eliminating a mortgage payment. Quite often someone will go into retirement, their house is not paid for, and they use assets to make their mortgage payment or pay off the balance. In this situation, I like using the Reverse Mortgage because it is an effective way to eliminate that mortgage payment and preserve those assets.

Very often, that same person hasn't retired and is still working because they are trying to get their house paid off. They will retire once it is paid off. So, a Reverse Mortgage gives one the ability to stay in their home for as long as they possibly can, but will not make the mortgage payment. Essentially, it turns your mortgage situation inside out. A Reverse Mortgage is a way we can still have a mortgage on our house, but not have to make the payment. This will preserve assets since they will not have to be used to create income for the payment or to pay off the mortgage.

The second way I use Reverse Mortgages is to provide a stream of income, usually for someone that is late in retiring and needs additional income. This is often a situation where people enter retirement with two Social Security benefits, and a death occurs. Remember, according to the Social Security widow rules, you're allowed to keep the higher of the married couple's two benefits, but not both. The house may present an attractive way to provide income through a reverse mortgage. I meet many seniors late in retirement who need additional income, or perhaps assets to repair the home and pay off credit cards or medical bills. They lack the assets necessary to do this, and need an additional source of income. A Reverse Mortgage could be a solution.

A third way I like to use the Reverse Mortgage is to provide a short- term, safe stream of income while waiting to file for Social Security. I encourage everyone to wait until age 70 before drawing benefits. A Reverse Mortgage is one possibility for drawing income while waiting until age 70 to file. It prevents the use of other assets to provide the income needed until filing.

Overall, the main way I use a Reverse Mortgage is to preserve assets and reduce liquidation costs. I want to preserve people's assets. I want their assets to continue to be invested and not be used for income, because whenever you use an asset, there's always a cost associated with using it. There are two types of costs associated with using an asset to provide income. One type of cost is a liquidation cost, which are the taxes associated with the use of that asset. For example, if you sell a stock or mutual fund, you might have to pay capital gains. If you take money out of an IRA to make a mortgage payment, you have to pay income taxes. Generally, there is always a cost associated with using an asset with some exceptions, such as a Roth IRA.

Whenever you use an asset, there is always a cost associated with its use. There's a cost to liquidate it. There's a cost to change it from one type of asset to an income. I want to avoid that liquidation cost. The costs associated with Reverse Mortgages are far less than the costs associated with taxes, whether they're capital gains or income taxes. That's why it is a way to preserve assets.

A second type of cost is opportunity cost. What is the future opportunity cost when you use an asset? If you take money out of an investment such as a stock or mutual fund, you've taken it out of whatever it's invested in. What is that future gain? What are you giving up over the years? Are you giving up a good stock or mutual fund that will grow?

A Reverse Mortgage does not affect the appreciation in your house. Your house will go up in value whether you have a mortgage or not. There will be a cost associated with using your equity, an interest cost, but that interest cost is far less than the taxes associated with it, or many times the opportunity costs. I like to use Reverse Mortgages to preserve assets and reduce liquidation costs.

The biggest reason people do not look at the Reverse Mortgage as a potential income solution is they have read that because of the costs associated with it, it is not a good deal. Closing costs typically are the reason why most people will not consider a Reverse Mortgage. It might be surprising for you to know that you can actually avoid most, if not all, of the closing costs associated with mortgages. You can't do it in every situation, but in many situations, this should not even be an objection to considering a Reverse Mortgage.

Even if those closing costs did exist, I would argue that they are less costly than taxes and the opportunity cost. To close this discussion of Reverse Mortgages, I want to give you a couple of technical details regarding the mechanics of Reverse Mortgage. I don't want to go into great detail about how exactly Reverse Mortgage works, but I want people to at least consider looking into it as a potential solution, and some basic correction of some misconceptions is helpful.

A common misconception with Reverse Mortgage is that the bank owns your home. This is not true. You have the title to your home. But, the bank does have an interest in your home, just like they would with any kind of traditional mortgage. The difference with a Reverse Mortgage is what triggers the payoff of the mortgage. With a traditional mortgage when you change ownership (title) you accelerate the payoff of the loan. You must pay it off. With a Reverse Mortgage, you actually have to pay back the Reverse Mortgage when the last person on the title leaves the home for twelve months or more, which generally happens because of death, or because they went into a nursing home. This is what makes it different than a traditional mortgage. The bank does not own you home in either situation.

If you pass away or leave the home for more than 12 months, the house would be put on the market and sold, and the Reverse Mortgage satisfied. Any additional money above what is owed would go to the estate and their beneficiaries. Reverse Mortgage companies actually send out a letter annually asking you to respond. If you don't respond to that letter, it tells them you no longer live in the house. They do this annually to make sure you are still alive and are still living in the home. This doesn't mean if you fell and broke your hip and had to go into rehab for two or three months the Reverse Mortgage would have to be repaid. You have to be out the home for more than a twelve-month period for that to happen.

One situation in which you should *not* consider a Reverse Mortgage is if you're thinking about downsizing. Quite often, when people talk about retirement, they talk about whether or not they want to downsize their home. They are not sure if they want to stay in the home, and may want to reduce the upkeep expenses or property taxes. If they need to downsize, that would be a situation in which a Reverse Mortgage would not be a solution. You don't have to absolutely know you're going to live in the home forever, but you should be reasonably certain you will remain for a while.

To summarize, the best way to provide safe income for retirement is to maximize the Social Security benefits you receive for your lifetime. And maximize the pension benefits you or your spouse will receive for your lifetime. You also need to create your own private pension plans through Immediate Annuities. Consider a Reverse Mortgage as an additional way to provide a safe income.

Another idea along these lines would be to reduce your taxes. Obviously, this is not a way to create income safely, but if we know some basic tax strategies for reducing the amount of taxes paid on our income, our spendable income will be increased. You might want to get some further help from your accountant or your adviser because there might be some ways you can maximize the after-tax income you receive in retirement.

One idea would be to consider a Roth conversion. There are two situations that could be very beneficial for people in this situation. There are two types of IRAs: a regular IRA, and a Roth IRA. A regular IRA is an IRA in which pre-tax contributions were made over your lifetime, so that when you make withdrawals, you pay income taxes. A Roth IRA is an IRA in which you make after-tax contributions, but you also have tax-free withdrawals.

There's also an option of doing what is called a Roth conversion. A Roth conversion is where we re-characterize a regular IRA to a Roth IRA. We do this because it gives us ways to receive tax-free withdrawals. The negative is that when we do a Roth conversion, we actually pay taxes on the fair market value of the asset that's being converted. Is it worthwhile to pay taxes on the market value of your IRA now so you can make tax-free withdrawals for your lifetime?

That's the tax planning situation associated with a Roth conversion. Understanding Roth conversion to determine whether not it is a good idea for you is a very complex matter that requires a CPA, it's not something most people can determine on their own.

Here are the two situations where I found the most benefit to converting a conventional IRA to a Roth IRA. The first situation occurs when someone goes into retirement, and it's clearly understood that they will use their IRAs as the largest provider of retirement income. I know that's a rather unusual statement, but many people go into retirement and do not use their IRAs as their primary source of retirement income. In fact, most people don't even take money out of an

IRA until they are required to do so, when they are 70.5 years old.

If the IRA is the primary asset to provide income, you may benefit from creating tax-free income from a Roth conversion. In my opinion, a Roth conversion will not benefit someone who will only take money out for emergencies, or when they reach the age of 70.5. In my opinion, people in those situations would be better off leaving the IRA where it is. But the fact that you will be using the Roth IRA for income over retirement, creating a tax-free stream of income over a long period of time is helpful and justifies the tax conversion costs.

The second situation in which I think people should look at a Roth conversion is when the market is down. Because you pay taxes on the fair market value of the IRA, when the market is down, taxes are minimized. In 2008, we discussed Roth conversion with many clients. Even though the stock market has come back since 2008, the growth associated with the rebound has not been taxed. So, the down market creates a more favorable environment in which to consider a Roth conversion. It doesn't necessarily have to be a down market for me to recommend Roth conversion, but it certainly helps.

Another tax reduction idea is to use capital gains for lump sum needs. For example, if someone needs to purchase a car or they have a large improvement or repair that needs to be made to the house, they will often take a withdrawal from their IRA. That withdrawal is considered income, so it's more favorable if you were to withdraw from an asset like a stock or a mutual fund that has capital gain treatments. Currently, capital gains are taxed at about half of the rate for income. It's a simple idea, but often ignored.

For those who worked for employers who have publicly traded stock, everyone needs an understanding of "net unrealized appreciation" or NUA. When people reach retirement, they will roll retirement plans into an IRA. But they will also combine publicly traded stock for the company they worked for together with other types of investments (like mutual funds) that they have been accumulating for retirement.

That's a big mistake because you have to keep them separate. You have to be able to keep company stock in one IRA account and keep all the other stock in a different IRA. When you withdraw money from the company stock IRA, the money is actually taxed as a capital gain vs. taxable income. If you put it all together, it will be taxed as income on the entire amount, which means you are going to double the amount of taxes that would have been associated with using stock. This is called Net Unrealized Appreciation. With NUA, you will be allowed to sell publicly traded stock for the company that you worked for, and receive capital gains treatment as opposed to ordinary income.

Another area where people pay unnecessary income taxes is with Non-Qualified Annuities. A Non-Qualified Annuity is very similar to a Roth IRA with after-tax contributions made to it. Tax is paid when you withdraw funds. Non-Qualified Annuities have a unique tax treatment. When you withdraw from a Non-Qualified Annuity it is taxes as income first. You pay income tax on the interest until all that is exhausted, and then it is considered principal.

For example, you might put $50,000 into a Non-Qualified Annuity that increases to $200,000 over the years. When you withdraw money, the first $150,000 that you withdraw will be considered interest income, and after $150,000 is withdrawn the rest is considered principal and not taxed.

One way to avoid this situation would be to annuitize. A Non-Qualified Annuity can be turned into an Immediate Annuity, where you take an income for some period. But by annuitizing it and not withdrawing it, you can treat a portion of that amount as principal and a portion of it as interest. You would be able to spread out the taxes over a longer period as opposed to paying taxes on all the income first. When you do this, the insurance company will also provide you with what's called an exclusion ratio, which is a number you can provide to your accountant indicating what percentage of the payments received are principal, and what percentage is considered interest. The negative associated with doing this is that, once you do this, you lock in the income and lose the use of principal. This should not be used in a withdrawal situation where you only want to withdraw money every now and then. It should not be used for a situation where you might pull a certain amount of money out one month, then six months later you pull another amount of money.

Another potential negative tax situation people run into is with life insurance. Most people buy life insurance to protect someone dependent upon them. If the policy holder is no longer here, the dependent will receive the policy holder's life insurance benefits for continued income. However, many people purchase life insurance as a way of providing retirement income, based on the theory that they can take tax-free withdrawals. In those situations, unfortunately, the insurance agent may omit several key points. The most important thing the agent may not tell you is that when you take these tax-free withdrawals, you must make sure the insurance policy stays enforced. It cannot lapse. If that insurance policy lapses, it creates a taxable event. Unfortunately, I see situations where the insurance agent does not tell the policy holder that the cash value in the policy is going to run out. If that happens before the policy holder dies, the policy will lapse. The withdrawals above your tax basis have to be reported as income.

A lapse in insurance policy often happens very late in life of the insured. What happens is the policy will have a substantial amount of cash value when the holder was younger. This gives a false sense of security. When they got older, the cost associated with the insurance coverage skyrocketed, eating up the cash value. The insured did not realize how much cash needed to be left in the policy to cover these costs. This fact surprises people, and it could put them in a situation where they may have to pay a large premium payment, late in life, to keep the policy enforced. If the policy holder doesn't pay the premium, the policy will lapse and they will incur a mess of taxes.

This is further complicated by the fact that by the time all this happens, the insurance agent who sold you the policy is usually long gone and no one is paying attention. Usually lapses in policies take place very late in retirement, when the insurance costs become significant and the agent is retired. At that point, there is no agent around keeping an eye on the policy.

If you purchased a policy as a source of retirement income, then you must make sure you have a current insurance agent with whom you can review the policy at least on an annual basis, to determine if the withdrawals are too aggressive. You don't want the insurance company to send you a letter saying your policy is about to lapse and you need to come up with $10,000 to keep it going. If you don't pay it you will receive a large 1099.

The last tax saving idea is called a QLAC. QLAC stands for "Qualified Longevity Annuity Contract." This is another type of annuity that I view favorably. A QLAC is used to minimize the required IRA distributions that are necessary when you reach age 70.5. Often, someone only takes money out when they reach 70.5 to avoid the penalties. A QLAC is a way that we can take a portion of our IRA, set it aside, and avoid the withdrawal rules. It's a way that we can minimize the required distributions. You might want to look into a QLAC if you have an IRA and you would like to minimize how much money you have to take out to avoid the penalties.

Chapter 7 Summary

- **Immediate Annuities are a great way to create lifetime income on your own.**

- **Reverse Mortgages are great ways to create safe income and preserve assets.**

CHAPTER 8

Emergency Assets

The next category in the bucket approach is Emergency Assets. Remember the qualities of Emergency Assets.:

- Accessible for emergencies such as a medical event or the death of a spouse.

- Not as liquid as Spendable Assets.

- Control taxation of the interest.

Because Emergency Assets are not as liquid as Spendable Assets, they may have a higher rate of return. When you are able to control whether or not you pay taxes on any interest accumulation earned, you will increase your rate of return over time through compounding. You want to be able to control the taxes so you only have to pay them when you use the assets. This will leave more in your account to grow as much as possible.

My favorite assets to be used for emergency funds are long-term CDs that contain free surrender privileges. There's a relationship in the financial world between liquidity and rate of return: the less liquid, the higher the rate of return. That's why you find a five-year CD pays more money than a six-month CD. When you have a long-term CD, you have the opportunity to receive a higher interest rate. The key is to have the free surrender privilege.

When you surrender a CD before it reaches maturity, you forfeit the interest earned. From time to time, the banks offer CDs that can invade the principal before maturity in the event of an emergency, but you will not incur a forfeit of interest. Emergency withdrawal is not something you can do regularly or monthly, but is something you can generally do one time and surrender the principal. These are the situations where you might set aside $25,000 in a CD, and then you might have an emergency bill and need to go into the CD before it matures to pay that medical bill. This is a great way to provide for Emergency Assets while tying principal up and receiving higher interest. The problem is that these types of CDs are not readily available or easy to find.

My next favorite way to provide for Emergency Assets is through a home equity line of credit. This is a bit of an unusual idea, so let me explain. When people come to me for retirement planning discussions, they usually have a lot of equity in their house that is just sitting there unused.

These are people who are not looking to downsize, so they might want to consider a Home Equity Loan. I describe a Home Equity Loan as a bank account tied to your home's value. Home equity has no bearing on the appreciation of your property. Your real estate will go up in value whether you have equity or not. The equity that is sitting in your account, in your house, is not being used, thus not bringing any kind of rate of return. I would like to access that home equity for emergencies.

The idea of a Home Equity Loan is to set up an equity line of credit that can be used in emergencies, which we can do with banks for little to no closing costs. The Home Equity Line of Credit just sits there until we need it. I like the use of a Home Equity Line because it allows us to use some of your home equity in those situations and not tie up other assets that are devoted to the emergencies. Home Equity Line is a great way to do that. Obviously, there's a cost associated with using the money in a Home Equity Loan, and this is a short-term situation. If you have taken assets that are *not* being used for emergencies and invested them for the long term, the only situation where you would not be able to use those assets for these emergencies is when the market is down.

For example, in 2007, you could have set up an Equity Line of Credit for emergencies, and instead of using assets set aside for emergencies you could have invested them in long-term growth. In 2008, if you had an emergency, you would have found it would not have been a good time to sell your stock or mutual funds. In that situation, you could go to the Home Equity Loan, get the temporary money you needed, wait for the market to return, and then pay off the Home Equity Line.

My next favorite way to provide for emergencies is with an Equity Index Annuity and the Long-Term Care Annuity. The Equity Index Annuity is an annuity in which the principal is guaranteed, and you receive an interest rate that correlates to the Standard & Poor's stock market index. As the stock market rises, you receive a percentage of that increase. If the stock market goes down, you won't lose your principal. Because it is guaranteed, it's only going to go in a positive direction. You might not make any money because the stock market is down, but you're not going to lose principal because the stock market's down either. This is a great alternative to bonds or CDs because it gives us the ability to receive higher rates of return when the stock market is good, but not have a downside risk associated with it.

You're not going to receive exactly what the stock market returns are on an Equity Index Annuity; you're going to generally receive about 75% of that. I think that's okay because I'd rather have 75% of the upside with no downside. Equity Index Annuities give you the ability to set aside an asset that can grow conservatively with no fear of the loss of principal. You can still receive a rate of return and control the taxation.

With annuities, one must be fully aware of the limitations on withdrawals, as well as other associated risks. Those are things that must be researched carefully. In general, when you purchase an Equity Index Annuity, it will have surrender charges for around five to seven years. That means if you put principal in, you can't immediately turn around and withdraw your principal without paying a cost to the insurance company. However, most annuities allow you to pull out at least 10% of the market value of the annuity every year. If you put in $100,000, you would be able to pull out $10,000 every year without penalties with under the surrender period. Or, you also would be able to annuitize the lump sum and take an income and turn it into an Immediate Annuity. I think Equity Index Annuities are a great way to safely provide an asset that can be easily converted into income and provide for emergencies.

One situation where the Equity Index Annuity is not a very good idea is when you expect to have emergencies that exceed the 10% withdrawal amount allowed while the annuity is under surrender periods.

If you are in a situation where there are lots of medical bills potentially coming, the Equity Index Annuity is probably not something you should consider. You need to be careful about the need for principal access during the surrender period.

The Long-Term Care Annuity is very similar to the Equity Index Annuity because the principal is guaranteed, and there will be some kind of interest rate associated with it. Both Equity Index and Long-Term Care Annuities have an insurance component. They make an increased amount available to you in certain medical situations, such as long-term care. You can easily convert these annuities into income even during the surrender period. This is what makes these Equity Index or Long-Term Care Annuities unique. Many companies offer them with increased income if someone needs long-term care. There is actually an increased income amount that's received in those care situations. To qualify for the insurance, you have to meet conditions referred to as the "Activities of Daily Living".

Activities of Daily Living, or ADL, are the industry standard for determining whether or not someone is eligible to receive long-term care benefits. Several activities make up our life, and if we lose the ability to do those activities, we would be considered as needing long-term care. These include activities such as taking medicine, feeding ourselves, dressing, bathing, and taking care of ourselves in general. These are the various activities of daily living.

One risk associated with these types of annuities is the financial stability of the insurance company. It needs to be carefully considered. You must research the strength of the company, just like with Immediate Annuities.

Under certain circumstances, there's an opportunity to switch existing annuities and insurance policies to these long-term care annuities. Often, I will see people who have held an insurance policy for a long time. It has cash value, and sometimes it was purchased by their parents many, many years ago. These insurances can be used and exchanged for a policy a little more appropriate for someone's needs in retirement, such as a policy that covers long term care. You may find older policies do not have the features of the latest generation of policies that cover long term care. There may be several advantages to finding out the details associated with the older policies, and possibly exchanging them. Recent policies have more long-term care benefits.

Finally, I want to mention an often-overlooked benefit for veterans. Currently, there is a benefit for veterans called the Aid and Attendance Benefit. Aid and Attendance Benefits are available to people age 65 or older who are 100% disabled. You're eligible for this if you were discharged from service with an Honorable Discharge, and you served 90 days or more with at least one day on active duty at a time of war.

You can visit the VA website and look up the different times when our country was at war. If you served at least one day on active duty during a war period, you are eligible for the Aid and Attendance Benefit. The Aid and Attendance Benefit is there for home healthcare, assisted living, and nursing homes. It is an excellent benefit. It is a pension benefit that many veterans don't even know is available to them, or for which they think they are not eligible. There is a good bit of planning needed to make someone eligible for this benefit that is beyond the scope of this book, but I wanted to mention it because we are talking about Emergency Assets. The Aid and Attendance

Benefit for veterans can be an excellent way to avoid having to use any assets. For more information, I would encourage you to visit the VA website.

Chapter 8 Summary

- **CDs with one time surrenders are a great way to save for emergencies.**

- **Equity Index Annuities and Long-Term Care Annuities are also great ways to obtain safe returns while remaining liquid for emergencies.**

CHAPTER 9

Long-Term Assets

The third bucket associated with retirement planning is long-term investments. If you have set aside sufficient money to produce spendable income and provide for emergencies, then you must also look at setting aside investments for the long-term. This is often overlooked by people in retirement, and it is probably the most important part of retirement planning.

Retirees need to understand they will spend many long years in retirement, and they cannot keep all of their money in a safe investment that earns barely any interest for all those retirement years. They must invest for the long-term. We could spend as many years in retirement as we do working. In 20 years, normal inflation will erode half of the purchasing power of our money. We need to have investments to keep up with that. Where do we find them?

Throughout history, the only place we have been able to grow our money was through the stock market, and the stock market makes retirees very uncomfortable. I certainly understand why. The most recent economic period of 2008 caused a lot of concerns for retirees. I hear a lot of questions, such as: Will an economic period like 2008 happen again? Will we ever recover? What about the government's debt? What are they going to do about Social Security? Should I be concerned about interest rates rising? How can I find safe money? Will real estate ever be the same? What is the upcoming election going to do? Retirees have a lot of reasons to be concerned.

I find the reason this area is so difficult for seniors is that they understand they are facing a long life expectancy, and the likelihood that government will shift more of the care burden to them. But the real enemy of retirement is inflation. The solution for this situation is very difficult to stomach. While everyone may realize they might be at risk of being frail and needing help, in order to invest in the stock market, one must be able to ignore the short-term fluctuations in place of long-term success. This is extremely difficult for seniors. They've worked their entire life, and they've accumulated assets they don't want to lose.

When we go through a period like 2008 with so much uncertainty, it's difficult to watch our assets fluctuate. Remember, no matter how bad it was during those times, the stock market always came back. The real question became: How long did it take to recover? The mistake most people make is they're not patient enough to wait for the recovery to happen. They sell at the wrong times out of fear. The longer you can wait during those periods, the less likely you will be to lose your principal.

But waiting for the recovery is extremely difficult for the senior, which is why I take the bucket approach. If you set aside enough assets to provide for current income, income that you need every single month, you have that guaranteed element, whether through Social Security, Immediate Annuities, or pension. You know that money will be there every time you need to buy groceries or pay for any other regular expense.

You should also set aside enough assets to provide for emergencies, expenses that are over and above the monthly. For example, you might have access to home equity through a Home Equity Loan. In that situation, you should not be fearful about setting aside additional assets for long-term growth. Because the need to sell assets invested in the stock market at the wrong time is minimized, if you don't need the money for short-term expenses, there is a greater likelihood you will be able to wait for the economy to recover and, therefore, not lose the principal.

This is so hard for people to do. That's why I like the balanced approach. I encourage people to set aside money for spendable assets, set aside money for emergencies, but also to set aside money for long-term growth. The security of your retirement depends upon how much of your assets you set aside for the long term because of the sheer number of years we spend in retirement. The more assets you can set aside to grow for the long-term, the more secure your retirement is going to be, and the less likely you will be to outlive your assets or be dependent upon someone else to take care of you when you become frail. Retirees cannot afford to leave all their money in banks and CDs with conservative interest rates that are not going to increase above inflation. While you may find the largest portion of your assets is in the income-producing basket or in the emergency basket, that's okay. It's important to set aside as much as you can in the long-term growth basket once those needs are met. There's never been a period in the stock market when this long-term approach has not worked, but it's difficult to weather the down periods.

One way I try to help my clients is by choosing stock market investments that are a bit easier to stomach. One of those investments is large company dividend stocks, or mutual funds. You can purchase a mutual fund or individual stocks with household name companies that have been around for a long time. Most people recognize these company names, and some companies have been around for 100 years or more. These companies pay very steady, very predictable dividends. As I mentioned in an earlier chapter, this is not the type of investment I generally recommend for income because of the fluctuations in principal, but I do think it's a very appropriate way to provide for growth. The steadiness and the predictability and the history of the dividend being reinvested give a reinvestment component to the growth of that asset. Over a long time, the reinvested dividend accumulates.

Household name company stocks and mutual bonds are excellent ways to provide for long-term growth in retirement. It's not the only way I use with my clients, but is probably my favorite way because people seem to understand and can identify with these large companies that have been around for a long time. It doesn't mean they can't lose money, but with proven dividend histories over a long time, they make a very significant and a very good way to invest for growth. You can do this individually with stocks, but I prefer to do it through mutual funds. Several different mutual funds focus on these types of companies. This is not a book about investments, but I want to mention the importance of setting aside as much as you can in growth or investments, and making sure you've taken care of your income needs and your emergency needs, so that whatever assets are devoted for the long-term, you can ignore the short-term fluctuations in the economy.

Chapter 9 Summary

- **Investing in large companies with long histories of dividends, either directly or through a mutual fund, is a great way to provide long term growth.**

CHAPTER 10

Miscellaneous Questions

Can a person lose Social Security benefits by working?

Yes, a person can lose some or all monthly benefits if he or she is under the Full Retirement Age (FRA) for all of 2019, and his or her earnings for the year exceed $17,040. A person may lose benefits if he or she reaches full retirement age in 2019 and if he or she earns over $45,360, but only those earnings earned before the month he or she reaches FRA count toward the $45,360 limit. The amount of loss depends on the amount of earnings in excess of these earnings limits. In no case will a person lose benefits for earnings earned after reaching FRA.

For purposes of this test, "earnings" include wages or earned income, and do not include unearned income, such as pensions, dividends, rental income or IRA withdrawals. It should be noted that benefits are not truly "lost", as benefits at full retirement age will be increased to account for benefits withheld due to later earnings.

Do Social Security benefits increase by continuing to work and contributing to Social Security?

It depends. When benefits are computed, Social Security uses the highest 35 years of earnings during age 22 through age 60. If the current earnings exceed the lowest year used in the computation, the benefits will increase. If the current earnings are less, then there will be no change.

What does "Full Retirement Age" (FRA) mean?

FRA means the age when people reach full retirement age. It depends upon your date of birth. See SSA.gov to see your FRA.

If you file for Social Security benefits early, how will later filings be affected?

The biggest filing mistake people make is failure to fully understand and take into account the impact of the new filing rules of 2015. When you file for a benefit, any benefit before your FRA, it will be reduced. Most people know this, but they do not know that later filings will also be reduced, even if it is after FRA and no longer early. For example, suppose you file for your benefits early while planning on filing later, such as in the case for spousal benefits. Even though you may not have filed early for the spousal benefit, it will be reduced as if you did. These are the new rules. They apply to all benefits, with the exception of widow benefits.

Is Social Security being cut?

The Social Security system's cost will exceed its income this year, the first time that has happened since 1982. This means current taxes do not support current benefits paid. The Social Security system is a "pay as you go" system, meaning benefits are dependent upon the collection of current payroll taxes. This year the Social Security trust fund surplus is being used to make up the difference between taxes collected and benefits paid. The Social Security surplus will run out in 2034. When this happens, benefits are expected to be decreased by 25% because current collected taxes only support 75% of benefits paid.

Many are under the impression the system will go bankrupt at some point, either by the time they retire, or during their retirement. That's simply untrue. While the program faces a funding shortfall by 2034, it is not going broke, because that would mean no one is paying payroll taxes. In other words, no one is working. If nothing changes with the current system, there will be a reduction of benefits, but the system is not going bankrupt. Changes would be required for the program to be able to pay full Social Security benefits. It is important to realize this is not the first time we have faced this problem.

In the 1970s we faced similar issues. We implemented the current retirement ages to fix the shortfall. In the past, full retirement age was 65 and then was delayed. I expect this to happen again. I believe there will be new delayed retirement dates for retirees. I also expect retirees to have to wait beyond age 70 for increased benefits. Another expected change is to eliminate the Social Security wage base. You may be familiar with the fact that you only pay Social Security taxes on a certain amount of income. We can expect to pay Social Security taxes on all income in the future.

Yes, Congress needs to solve the problem and does not seem to be in any rush to do so, but I believe they will get to it, probably at the last minute when everyone is screaming for a solution. They don't seem to have much desire to deal with it today.

How can I verify my benefit?

"MySocialSecurity" is a free online account that gives you quick and secure access to your personal Social Security information. You can set up an account by going to w.w.w.ssa.gov/myaccount."

What if I have a security freeze or a fraud alert on my credit report?

You cannot create a "MySocialSecurity" account online if you have a security freeze or fraud alert on your credit report. You first must ask to have the freeze or alert removed.

What is the maximum payable Social Security retirement benefit?

The maximum benefit depends on the age you retire. In 2018, if you retire at full retirement age, your maximum benefit is $2,788.00. However, if you retire at age 62 in 2018, your max benefit is $2,159, and the benefit will increase to $3,698 if you retire at age 70.

Will military retirement benefits affect Social Security benefits?

You can get both Social Security retirement benefits and military retirement benefits. Generally your Social Security benefits will not be affected by your military benefits.

If I get Social Security disability benefits and I reach full retirement age, will I then receive retirement benefits?

Social Security disability benefits automatically change to retirement benefits when disability beneficiaries reach full retirement age. You cannot receive both retirement and disability benefits on one earnings record at the same time. The amount will stay the same.

If I change my mind about filing, can I withdraw my Social Security retirement claim and reapply?

If you change your mind, you may be able to withdraw your Social Security claim and reapply at a future date. However, you must do this within 12 months of your original retirement.

Are the benefits withheld under the Earnings Test "lost"?

Any benefits withheld while you continue to work are not "lost". Once you reach NRA (normal retirement age), your monthly benefit will be increased to account for the months in which benefits were withheld.

What is Deemed Filing?

Monthly benefits grow larger for each month you delay receiving retirement benefits between your full retirement age (FRA) and age 70. Under existing law, if you are eligible for benefits both as a worker and as a spouse or divorced spouse, you will receive the higher of the two benefits. This requirement is called "Deemed Filing" because when you apply for one benefit you are "deemed" to have also applied for the other, whether you want it or not. You receive the higher of the two benefits.

Deemed filing means that when you file for either your retirement or your spouse's benefit, you are required or "deemed" to file for the other benefit as well, so you not be able to restrict which benefit is received. Remember: those born before 1954 should be aware of the restricted application and the ability to pick and choose which benefits they receive.

What is the "Normal Retirement Age" (NRA)? Below is listed how the Normal Retirement Age varies by year of birth.

Year of Birth	NRA
1937 and prior	65
1938	65 and 2 months
1939	65 and 4 months
1940	65 and 6 months
1941	65 and 8 months
1942	65 and 10 months

1943-54	66
1955	66 and 2 months
1956	66 and 4 months
1957	66 and 6 months
1958	66 and 8 months
1959	66 and 10 months
1960 and later	67

If my divorce is less than 2 years, will it affect benefits?

After 2 years of the date of filing, the age of the divorced spouse does not affect the person claiming benefits. Before 2 years the ex-spouse must be age 62 and filed.

Should I wait to file for divorced benefits or spousal benefits past FRA?

No. Delayed retirement credits apply only to your own benefit. The delayed retirement credits do not apply to benefits on someone else, such as a spouse or ex-spouse or deceased spouse. There is never an incentive to wait past FRA to file because benefits do not increase. Only your own benefit will increase to age 70.

Will re-calculation affect me negatively?

If your income after age 60 is less than one of the 35 years used to calculate your benefits, this will not reduce benefits. Recalculation will only help you, not hurt you.

ABOUT THE AUTHOR

Philip Wilson is a veteran financial advisor since 1989, and host of a weekly radio show on Social Security. He is a fee-only Alabama Registered Advisor located in Birmingham, Alabama. At the time of publishing this book, Philip was the only advisor certified in Social Security Claiming Strategies in Alabama; there are less than 50 certified advisors across the country. He lectures more than 50 times a year on the subject at local churches, libraries, places of business, and other venues across the state. For more information on Philip as a speaker, or to contact Philip, see www.ssmistakes.com.

Made in the USA
Coppell, TX
13 September 2021

62301242R00057